One God, One Truth

The Clear and Simple Evidence

by

Dwaine Canova

Table of Contents

Acknowledgements

There are many people whose lives and writings and teachings have impacted my walk with God and I am thankful for them. This page is set aside for those who have invested many hours of their personal lives encouraging me so that I was able to write this book.

Albie Pearson and his wife, Helen, have taught me more about the Bible and how to 'mine' it better than anyone else. Their lives and hearts are Jesus' earthly model for me. They have counseled me through years of learning how to become a father, husband, friend, and companion of Jesus through the power of The Holy Spirit.

Dr. Michael T. Jupina and his wife, Lynn have encouraged me for many years. Their friendship has been exhibited without limits.

With the exception of Jesus, my wife, Janet, is the most spectacular human being to exist on earth. Her support, encouragement, and love have nourished me through times of weakness and strength. She is a complete Proverbs 31 woman and wife.

My children, Laura and Matt Whitson, Ryan, and Stephen give me grace and joy beyond measure. They are truly God's gifts to Janet and me.

My brother Gary and his wife Virginia have encouraged and supported me beyond the requirements of a brother. I am thankful for them and their impact in my life.

Dewey and Donna James have demonstrated friendship, encouragement and support without measure.

Neil and Val Marshall, my wife's parents (and mine for 38 years), prayed for many years to get me back in fellowship with the Lord. Their encouragement and parenting have been an invaluable model for my life.

Sonja Brown has extended herself unselfishly to get this book pulled together so that it got to print. It would not have happened without her experience and commitment.

Many friends have read the manuscript and given input to improve the book. I am thankful for all they have done and mention them here in alphabetical order; Bill Knapp, Erica Madigan, Scott Peters, Steve Russomano, Dan Spencer, Lisa Villaluna, Tom Vitale, Sharon Williamson, and Steve Winum.

My God is my sustainer and my strength in all things. May this book, He has birthed and brought forth through me, be an encouragement to His Bride as she prepares for the Coming of Christ.

Introduction

*O*ne God, One Truth was written to answer questions—
the kind of questions that we've all asked. "Why do I
believe what I believe?" "What good does it do to believe
that way?" "Is there evidence to support a belief in Jesus
Christ or am I following blindly?" "What happens if I don't
decide to follow Christ?" "How can I know what is true?"

As you read, it is my hope that you will find the answers
to many of your questions about the life of faith. Of course,
I don't have all the answers—no one does—and I'm not a
properly trained theologian—who wants a lot of church
talk—but I can offer you the answers I've found after more
than forty-five years of searching, doubting, researching,
and speaking with many wise and knowledgeable people.
I've learned by reading voraciously, living intensely, and
questioning everyone and everything around me. Now, I
hope you can reap the benefits by simply listening to what I
have to say.

If you want to do some searching on your own, I encourage you to take advantage of the resources listed in the back
of this book. Even though I stand behind the answers I've
provided, it is always wise to seek confirmation through

your own study. My prayer is for you to be taught and stimulated to learn even more so you can teach and encourage others.

The Opening Conversation

"**D**ad, why are you a Christian?" My son is now a young adult with a great mind. The question is offered to challenge me, but with the hope that I have a good answer.

"I'm eager to share that with you," I tell him, "but I'll need a few hours of your time."

"I can't right now, Dad. But maybe tomorrow you could take me to lunch." I love the mischievous smile that follows the statement-question. Everyone in our family loves to talk over a meal, and it certainly is my favorite form of entertainment.

"I'd love to have lunch with you tomorrow. Do I get to pick the place?"

"Yes, you can pick Dad, and I know it will be a restaurant with Mexican food." The mischievous smile shines again.

"Great. We'll go to La Hacienda. It's my favorite, and I know you like it also."

"That works for me."

"Before you go though, may I give you the one-minute answer?" I want him to think about a few things before we tackle the big questions.

"Sure."

"First, the Christian Bible is the most accurate, authenticated, corroborated document of antiquity. It is a reliable source."

"And, you are certain of that?"

"Yes, I am very certain. And second, unlike any other book in the world, the two parts—Old Testament and New Testament—contain clear and specific prophecies that have been fulfilled and recorded as being fulfilled."

"How do you know they have been fulfilled?"

"I'll give you more detail tomorrow. And third, the fulfilled prophecies are supported by secular history, archaeology, and the work of experts who study ancient documents."

"You mean you're not going to tell me the Bible stories I already know?" I love the smile my son flashes when his intention is to lovingly agitate me or spur me on.

"Yes, I will tell you some Bible stories after you are certain the Bible is authoritative. I want you to take it very seriously—seriously enough to stake your life on it."

"If you are certain the Bible is a reliable source, why is there so much confusion and speculation about it?"

"The confusion exists because people either have incorrect information or they reject the truth because it doesn't fit their situation or lifestyle."

"Well it's more than that, isn't it?"

"Yes, there is more detail, but I think that's a fair summary."

"Dad, here are two thoughts in one question, which I'll leave with you so you can prepare for tomorrow. There are more than 6 billion people on the planet and only 1.5 billion claim to be Christians. Those 1.5 billion seem to have a very difficult time agreeing on what it means to be a Christian. If they're confused, how do they expect to get others to agree with them?"

"Those are very good thoughts. I look forward to talking with you about them. Come tomorrow with all your questions and assumptions. We'll have a great time."

We stand and hug. I very much enjoy hugging my adult children. It always causes me to recall hugging them in the first moments of their lives. Wow! What a blessing it is to have children to love. And what a miracle it is to know that God loves us—His children—even more than we love ours.

Dad's Story

I've spent most of my life trying to get ahead. "I'm making a name for myself," I would declare, "I want to make my family proud." Actually, I was making a name for myself so I could be proud of me, and I hoped others would be, as well. My underlying motivation was pride and ego.

As my children grew up, they lived with a father who was intense, volatile, self-centered and driven. I was more aggressive than most, and exhibited a very passionate commitment to my company and church. I focused on family only when I found the time. I'm very grateful that our children had their mother's influence to soften mine.

When the teen years arrived, our son began to assert himself, rebelling against everything he thought I stood for. It soon became apparent that he was using this means to express his hurt and punish me for failing him as a father.

This was a true awakening for me. I entered into counseling with Christian and non-Christian counselors and made many changes. My son is now a young adult and doing well. He is not interested in a business career, nor is he interested in church.

The lingering bad feelings about business could stem

from seeing the anguish and extra hard work and long hours I spent as an entrepreneur. The negative attitude about church could be the result of seeing my passion and intensity for working, reading, studying the Bible, and attending church functions—while feeling that I was not nearly as passionate and committed to him. My son was in his later teen years when the Lord changed my heart. My changed heart marked the beginning of my son's sense of love and acceptance.

In the early years, all of our children went to Christian schools and attended church regularly. We were at all the events and the children participated at every opportunity. The churches and the schools focused on discipline, and none of our children were a disciplinary problem until later in their school careers.

The sternness of church and school, along with the sternness of their father at home placed them in an uncomfortable position. The bright light in all this was their mother—a wonderful mom in every way. Unfortunately, she could not mitigate the pain they felt in the presence of their father. All she could do was contain it, help the children be disciplined, focus on the good times, and try to ignore the bad times.

In the end, God's grace was sufficient. My wife and I are now happily married. The children are all near by and we enjoy close relationships with them. I appreciate the hugs of my children more than any other physical thing on earth.

What caused the change in my heart? That's what I hope you will discover as you read this book. I'll share the things I wish I'd known as I started my relationship with Jesus—things that could have made my children's lives very different. I still cry uncontrollably, on occasion, when I remember their looks of fear, which I did not acknowledge or understand at the time. To them I was a man of God who prayed, read, studied, taught, and went to church. I was not the kind of man that Jesus was and wanted me to be.

I now know Jesus in an entirely new way. I have spent thousands of hours reading, studying, teaching, being taught, and praying for wisdom. I know there is only One God, and there is only one way to God, and that is Jesus. I'm confident that the information in this book and the resources listed at the end of this book will help you reach the same conclusion.

I've also learned that God can and will change lives for the better right here on earth. You won't have to wait to get to heaven to experience the value of having a personal relationship with Jesus. It is this reality that I'll be sharing. An exciting example is that my child will set aside a couple of hours to hear me talk about Jesus. Please read on and join us in this important conversation.

Son's Story

I'm looking forward to time with my dad tomorrow. He
has studied so diligently, and I'm proud that he has spent
the time to organize what he believes and why he believes it.
Too often I meet people who have strong opinions, but they
don't always have the discipline to study and learn so they
can speak with authority about why they believe as they do.

Being my dad's child was not all that easy. He was, and
still is, an incredibly intense guy. Sometimes that's good,
but many times, especially in my younger years, it was bad.
When I came home, I always wanted to know about Dad's
mood. If he was 'up', then we'd all be 'up', but if he was
struggling with an issue at work, then we all walked on
eggshells. Mom was very good about preparing us, so we'd
know when to be extra careful to avoid creating an incident.

Of course, we also had a lot of fun. Our vacations were
first class. We went to the best places, and we never had to
cut corners. We could take friends. In fact, we almost
always took friends. They really liked my dad, but they
didn't have to live with him all the time. Besides, he was
always at his best when other people were around.

Mostly I just felt confused. My dad could be so good

sometimes and so bad at other times. His moodiness and temper would flare up without notice and set all of us on edge. Those outbursts seemed to be quickly forgotten by him, but they made me feel afraid and deflated—mostly they made me feel bad about myself.

The time tomorrow with my dad will be good. We've been meaning to do this for some time. I've probably heard most of the stuff he's planning to share with me, but I'm ready to hear it again. He's now like an old professor. He loves to discuss and teach and encourage. I know he won't get angry if I disagree. I know he is very intense about all this. He is as intense as he's always been, but he does it now with a softness that is firm and a gentleness that doesn't speak of weakness. I think the big difference now is that it is not about him. For him, it's about me. He loves me, and he loves sharing his love for Jesus, who is very real and present for him.

This will be a mountaintop event tomorrow. It's been long in coming, and I'm eager to be there.

The Proper Attitude

❧

We arrive at the restaurant as the lunch rush is drawing to a close. There are available tables that will not be needed until the evening meal—no need to rush our conversation.

After we settle in at the table, my son speaks. "I love it here at La Hacienda. The place is clean, not too fancy, and the food is great. I know there are many varieties and styles of Mexican food, but this is the best. I know this has been your favorite since you were a kid, Dad, but it's also mine."

"I'm glad it's your favorite too. It gives us one more thing to share. And, I like sharing favorite things with you. We've learned a lot together, and I'm sure we're going to learn even more together."

The waiter arrives to take our order. "I'll have two tacos and a special quesadilla with a large order of refried beans," my son says.

"And, for you Señor?" asks the waiter.

"I'll have the taco plate with beans only. Queso cotija, por favor. It is my favorite cheese for Mexican food."

"Okay, Dad, we're having our favorite food in our favorite place, and we're going to be talking about your favorite topic." He smiles. "Are you happy now?"

"Oh yes, I'm deliriously happy. Talking and eating is my favorite form of entertainment."

We both laugh loudly, but since it's late in the lunch hour and the restaurant is practically empty, we doubt that anyone will mind.

I get right to it.

"First I want to establish my motive and, second, an important constraint. My motive is that you will know, understand, and love Jesus as passionately as I do. I have enough data and evidence to convince you intellectually, but it still starts in the heart and comes as a gift. Our God is a gentleman. He will never force Himself on you. He waits to be invited. So, there'll be no attempt at force here either."

"And the constraint?"

"The constraint is that as I explain to you why I believe as I do, it must be done logically, courteously, and with respect for you and others. Even though my opinion might be different from someone else's, I mean no disrespect. I'm sure I'll make that point more than once today, but it is very important."

"Why is that so important?"

"Well, that's the way Jesus would do it, and that's the way the Bible tells us to do it. I also feel that if I had been born into a different family or in another part of the world, I would probably believe differently than I do now. Most of us are heavily influenced by our family heritage and the culture in the place where we grow up. There is no way I could be indignant or feel negatively about anyone since I believe they are mostly products of circumstances outside of their control. I'm thankful for my birth and the path the Lord has taken me so that I would come to know him. My opportunity now is to share this information with others so they might know that the God of Abraham, Isaac, and Jacob is the only God—and He is the only Truth."

"That's a pretty bold statement to make considering the diversity of people and religions in the world."

"Yes, I know it's bold, but more importantly, it's true. That's why we must share it properly, courteously, and with respect for others' circumstances. For me the clarification begins with the evidence contained in the primary books used by the various religions. Another consideration is how those books came into being. Such questions as 'how were they written', 'who wrote them', and 'are they accurate', . would be a good place to start."

"Then let's get started. Where would you like to begin?"

"I'm going to start with The Christian Bible. I want to start with the real thing, so we can use it as a standard against which we can measure and evaluate the others."

The Christian Bible

"As you know the Bible has two main sections; the Old Testament and the New Testament. The Old was written over a 1,000-year period by more than 35 different writers. The first writing is attributed to Moses, who wrote the first five books—the Pentateuch—around 1400 B.C. In these books, God describes how the world was created, and He also tells us about His relationship with Abraham and, ultimately, with the nation of Israel. The history runs from the beginning of time until the Israelites, the people of promise, are out of Egypt and on their way into the land promised them by God through Abraham."

"So, it covers a long period of time?"

"Yes, it covers a long period of time but includes the main points about the relationship God wanted to have with people; what He would do for them, and what He required of them."

"The Bible doesn't really answer all the questions there are about the creation of the world or the dinosaurs and things like that," my son challenges.

"It may not answer them easily or to your immediate satisfaction, but expert scientists, who are Christian in their beliefs, have studied the evidence and concluded that creation, as described in the Bible, is correct. But ... let's not try to solve this one right now. We can come back to it. I will refer you to some resources that I believe do a superb job of explaining all the detail. Just know, for now, that there is a mountain of evidence and research to support the creation story as described in the Bible."

The meals arrive at the table. We pray and begin to eat. Eating slows our conversation but it doesn't stop it.

"The food is great as always," my son says enthusiastically. "Okay, Dad, go on. I'll eat while you talk." We pause for a laugh.

"The next books of the Old Testament cover the period from around 1400 B.C. to 400 B.C. These books contain the history, poetry, and prophecies of the Israelites and the peoples with whom they came in contact. These books contain great teaching and great prophecies. Some of the prophecies were actually fulfilled within the period of the writings; some of them were not fulfilled until after the Old Testament writings were completed, and some have not yet been fulfilled. These fulfilled prophecies are also corroborated by non-biblical writings and archaeology."

"Why is that so important?"

"As we get further into this, you'll see that the accuracy of prophecies, as supported by archaeology and secular history, is one of the things lacking in the books used by other religions."

"What is secular history?"

"In this context it refers to writings and points of history that are not related to nor concerned primarily with religion."

"So, some of the things in the Bible are supported by writing and events outside the Bible?"

"That's right."

"Then why don't preachers and teachers of the Bible make this known?"

"They do, but people aren't always listening. Also, the preachers and teachers are so aware of it and so familiar with it that they sometimes forget that this evidence is not as well known to their listeners. They begin with the premise that the Bible is the complete and accurate words of God to man and expect other people to believe this, as well.

The people they are leading, however, sometimes develop doubts about the authority, accuracy, and authenticity of the Bible when they get to tough places in their lives or they are tempted and distracted by the things of the world. Also, I think when people want to do what they know they should not, they conveniently do all they can to explain away the thinking and guidelines that conflict with what they want to do. Not all misbehaving children are two years old."

We both laugh. No doubt we have different memories running in our minds, but the entertainment value is still there.

"So people who attend church *should* know these things?" asked my son.

"Yes, I bet most people know some or all of this, but it doesn't get brought to the front of their minds that often."

"Is it important for them to know?"

"I think it is. In our culture, we are constantly being bombarded with information, and particularly in this country, we feel great pressure to be accepting and tolerant of all things. This desire for tolerance has become almost a requirement. Popular thinking tells us that the more tolerant we are, the smarter and more enlightened we become. At the same time, our society seems to be attracted to rebellious ideas and people like a moth to a light. The media is very ready to publish and portray rebellious behavior and thinking in a positive way. These writers and newscasters believe, very sincerely, that they are entertaining us and helping us become a better society. Unfortunately, just the opposite is happening. We are becoming a weaker society.

Perhaps their intention is not to lead people astray, but that is certainly the result."

"Do you really believe we are becoming a weaker society? Look at all the advances in science, technology, and our ability to make life easier and better."

"I am aware of many of the advances, and they are marvelous. I started teaching computer programming in 1967. I've witnessed the advances in technology over the years. I've seen how that technology helped all fields of endeavor from medical research to space travel. I played golf with Alan Shephard, a man who literally went to the moon and back. It was a delight to talk with a person who had been a key part of a very impressive accomplishment using the latest technologies of his day. I love the new technologies, but I have to ask this question: Have they made our cities and homes better places to live than they were 40 years ago? What do you think?" I ask my son.

"I think there are issues, but life is easier for us now than it was for you or your dad. Think of all the things my grandfather didn't have. He didn't have technology to entertain him or make his job or life easier. And now the government no longer allows child labor or abuse. More people have access to more education than ever before. We have so much more than my grandfather had."

"Yes, but we also have a list of social ills that should not exist, given all that education and technology," I reminded him.

"Isn't the government supposed to take care of those?"

"I don't believe any government can fix these social ills. Too many bright, talented people are working at it, giving it their best, but the problems are still with us."

"Then what's the answer?"

"I think the answer lies within the nature of man. The answer to all this is for people to turn to God, love Him, and obey Him."

"That's it?" he protested.

"That's it."

"Isn't that a bit simplistic?"

"Yes, it's very simplistic, but it's true."

"I don't believe it's that simple."

"Let me offer this for your consideration. I know you remember how I was when you were growing up."

"Yes, I remember." He smiles.

"Try to imagine where we would be if I hadn't changed. Would we be speaking to each other? Would you be in turmoil somewhere with a heart full of bitterness and little or no ability to have an intimate relationship? How would that make your life different?"

"I'm not sure," my son ventures hesitantly.

"I'm sure you would not have the solid relationships you have now, and you would be doing many things to numb or temporarily remove the bitterness in your heart. And, you would very likely be doing things that are not good for you."

"You could be right."

"I know I'm right and there are truckloads of documents and real-life stories to support my thinking. The answer is Jesus. My relationship with Jesus and the understanding of how He heals and changes hearts was vital to my change."

We both pause and think silently for a while. The waiter comes and refills our glasses.

"Okay, let's get back to the Bible."

"A point I'd like to make about the Old Testament is that contained in it are 61 specific prophecies about Jesus that are documented as happening in the life of Jesus of Nazareth. These prophecies were rendered 1400 to 400 years before He was born. That would be equivalent to many past generations of our relatives predicting the details . of the life of the quarterback for the winning Superbowl in the year 2500 A.D. It is simply not possible. A phenomenon like this occurred only once and is documented in the

Christian Bible. This is a powerful piece of evidence that must be considered."

"You mean there are 61 prophecies about Jesus and they all happened?"

"Yes, they all happened. Some scholars list more than 100 prophecies, but I've stayed with the list provided by Josh McDowell in his book *The New Evidence that Demands a Verdict.*"

"Who is Josh McDowell?"

"Josh McDowell is a wonderful teacher and researcher. His book provides evidence as a resource for college students who wish to defend their belief in Jesus. He is very well known in many Christian circles, but his work is not used enough to suit me. He also wrote a book called, *More Than a Carpenter*, which is in great demand all over the world—especially in Muslim countries where people are being freed from their oppressive governments. It is also a great book for providing answers for the skeptic and the weak believer."

"What do you mean by 'weak believer'?"

"Many people believe in Jesus, but they have unanswered questions that lead to doubt and anxiety. They are not as strong as they need to be to resist the lure of the world around them. When they get into rough places—as we all do—they don't have a firm conviction that God will take care of them. The society we live in adds to that doubt through all the media and the influence of non-believing friends."

"Are weak believers saved?"

"They are saved, but they don't fully enjoy their relationship with Jesus through the power of the Holy Spirit."

"What do you mean by 'fully enjoy'?"

"Imagine being in a relationship you weren't sure you should be in and trying to make the most of it. Those are difficult relationships. At times you think you should get out and, yet, you're afraid to get out."

"Why are people afraid to get out?"

"For many it is because they are just not sure if there is or isn't a real and active God. They don't want to take a chance if it's true. Others are afraid they'll disappoint their friends or families. In both cases, they are just not as definite about their belief as they would like to be and should be."

"How can they change it so they have a strong belief?"

"They need to know without hesitation or doubt that the Bible is the complete and accurate words of God to mankind. They need to read these words and ask to be taught by these words through the Holy Spirit. They need to attend a church that teaches from and uses the Bible as the sole authority. The church should also provide an environment where they can be encouraged, nurtured, and have close, supportive friendships."

"Dad, I want to get back to the Bible now. How do we know the prophecies were fulfilled as stated in the New Testament? I think that is pretty powerful if it's true, but how can I know it's true?"

"The truth of this lies with the circumstances under which the New Testament was written. The New Testament is the most accurate, authenticated, corroborated document of antiquity. I can make that claim not only by using information from the Bible but also from the work of scholars who study old documents.

"Consider these facts:

"Homer's *Iliad* was written around 800 B.C. The earliest copies that exist today date to around 400 B.C. That means there is a 400-year gap from the time it was written until we have copies that can be used to confirm the accuracy of the writing. There are 643 copies and portions.

"*Plato* was written around 400 B.C. and the copies available today date to 900 A.D. That means there is a 1300-year gap from writing to having copies. There are just seven copies of Plato.

"The New Testament was written in 50 to 100 A.D. and the date of copies is from 114 A.D. to as late as 325 A.D. That means there is, at the outside, a 275-year gap with some having a gap of less than 75 years from the writing until we have copies. There are more than 24,000 copies and portions.

"These statistics for the New Testament are incredible. There are more copies from a shorter elapsed time than any other document of antiquity. This leads one to a high degree of certainty that the copies we use today are accurate from the original teachings and writings. Also, remember that the writers of the New Testament are eyewitnesses who wrote about their experiences."

"Those are impressive and confusing statistics," my son protested. "Can you give that all to me one more time?"

I repeat the information again a little slower and with emphasis on the numbers for the gaps of time and the copies for the various documents. I wait for my son to acknowledge that he has registered all of it. I repeat some things a third time.

"How does this compare with other old documents?"

"Homer's *Iliad* is second, with the New Testament being first and then there are a host of other books of antiquity with most having only a few copies dating 400 to 1,500 years from the time of the original writings. It is very impressive information authenticating the accuracy of the Bible."

"Yes, it is impressive from that standpoint, but how will all that affect my thinking?"

"Assuming that a person is going to believe anything, he or she must have a reliable source of information. In addition to being accurate, this most reliable source also contains prophecies that were written hundreds of years before they were fulfilled—very accurately fulfilled, I might add. There is no other book or compilation of books like this anywhere else in the world."

"I need to think about the full implications of that."

"While you're thinking, let me also tell you that the writers of the New Testament were either eyewitnesses or received their information from eyewitnesses. These were not the writings of historians, but people who were there, on the scene, reporting what they were seeing and hearing. Many of these writers started out as skeptics or even openly opposed to believing that Jesus was who He said He was. When I read the New Testament, I read it as though I am reading an ancient newspaper filled with articles and letters written by witnesses who are giving their firsthand accounts of what they heard, observed, or experienced."

"So, the writers either were with Jesus or personally knew people who were with Jesus and had experiences with Him?"

"Yes, and there is a statement to consider in a book by David Bentley-Taylor, who wrote about a Jewish historian by the name of Josephus Flavius." I reach into my briefcase and just happen to have a copy of Mr. Bentley-Taylor's book with a marker on page 73.

"Josephus was a historian born only five or six years after Jesus was crucified and rose from the dead. He lived from about 37 A.D. to about 101 A.D. He wrote extensively, and in his book, entitled *Jewish Antiquities,* he wrote these words: 'Now there was about this time Jesus, a wise man, if it be lawful to call him a man, for he was a doer of wonderful works, a teacher of such men as receive the truth with pleasure. He drew over to him many of the Jews and many of the Gentiles. This man was Christ. And when Pilate, at the suggestion of the principal men among us, had condemned him to the cross, those that loved him at the first did not forsake him, for he appeared to them alive the third day, as the divine prophets had foretold these and ten thousand other wonderful things concerning him. And the tribe of Christians, so named after him, are not extinct at this day (18:3:3).'"

I paused to give this time to sink in.

"This is a valuable piece of evidence—a historian who lived near the time of the early Church stating that Jesus' life and the things He did were well known. Jesus is confirmed by a non-biblical source of history as a real person who existed and did the things recorded in the Bible. Josephus is not listed in the Bible, so it is not wrong to assume he was very likely not involved as a leader in the early Church. Also, his extensive writings would have kept him busy."

"I like this. So, this non-Christian historian made these statements in a non-religious book of history. He wrote this in the first century A.D. around the time of the Jesus Bible stories?"

"Yes."

I give him time to think about this and wait for more questions.

Finally he spoke. "So, there is a lot of evidence surrounding the life of Jesus, and a lot of data to support the authenticity of the New Testament. What about the Old Testament?"

"The Old Testament for the Christian community is the Scripture used, even today, by those who practice Judaism. The Jewish Scriptures were translated into the Greek language around 250 B.C. and they've been used in that form since that time. Also, there are many instances in the New Testament where Jesus refers to the 'Scriptures' as the source of His teaching. Eyewitnesses corroborate the truth and reality of Jesus, and in His teachings, Jesus refers to and corroborates the truth and teachings of the Old Testament or Jewish Scriptures."

"So, in the Old Testament there are prophecies about Jesus, which He fulfilled. And while He was on earth, He quoted from and used the same Scriptures that Jews used at that time and still use today?"

"That is correct. By doing so He authenticates the Old Testament as being integral to the complete understanding of God."

"I like that."

"I like it too. Where is there another book like this with two parts so intricately welded together in teachings and history and archaeology and relevance for today? Where is there another single volume that has prophecies fulfilled and documented?"

"I guess there is no other," my son concedes.

"You don't have to guess. You can be certain there is no other. And that is another reason why I base all my beliefs on what I read in the Old and New Testaments."

"So, Dad, you have done your homework. I know you have many more details you could share, but we're just skimming the surface, right?"

"Yes, you're correct; this is just a summary that covers the essentials in a very basic way."

"What if someone wanted to study all these things you have studied? How long would it take?"

"Well, I've spent a lot of time, but the real work was done by many people and I've just read some of the summary work from Josh McDowell, Lee Strobel, Ravi Zacharias, and others who are the real scholars. They have researched and used the work of other scholars, as well. One could read any of their books in a few hours and come away with a deep understanding."

"How many books have they written?"

"Josh McDowell has written at least 45 books. Lee Strobel has written at least four. Ravi Zacharias has written five to ten books. I recommend them highly."

"Do I need to read all 50 or 60 books?"

"No, but if you read a couple of them, you'll be encouraged to read others. These are very good books written by wonderful godly men who have interesting personal histories and lives. Only one of them was a Christian in the early part of his life. They are all well educated. They each went through a period of being a skeptic or atheist who opposed

Christianity. As they worked to dismiss Christianity intellectually, they became firm believers and are now teachers and writers skilled at presenting the truths of Christianity."

"Is that why you recommend them?"

"Yes—partly because of what they went through but also because they might not have written such great books and been such good teachers if they had not been intensely opposed to Christianity for a period of time. In addition, they all have personal changes in their lives that attest to the reality of the active workings of Christ today. All three are currently alive and understand the circumstances of the present time. That is also an important qualification."

"They are living examples. Is that what you're trying to say?"

"Yes."

"So, how would you summarize all this?"

"When I hold the Bible in my hands I am certain I am holding a book containing the foundational truths for the universe. I am sure it is God's inspired writings. I'm certain it is inspired because the frequent and accurate foretelling of the future could not have occurred without the influence of God. Also, the writers readily admit their relationship and dependence upon God. It is written down for us so that we can know Him and know that God knows each one of us individually. There are many things about God that are still a great mystery to me, but I know He loves me personally. I know I can rely on Him daily in this life. And I know that I have an incredible eternity waiting for me thanks to Him. That gives me a lot of comfort and confidence for each day and forever."

We ask the waiter to bring more iced tea and watch in silence as our empty plates are removed. It is time to take a break.

Christianity's Confusion

We reconvene at the table just as the waiter is leaving us a bowl of fresh chips. I can sense a new area of questioning coming. My son seems impressed by the information about the Christian Bible, but there are still many unanswered questions.

"Well, Dad, I am swayed by your information about the Bible," he begins, "but what about all these other religions and even the confusion and disagreement within the groups of people who claim to be Christians? I don't see how there can be all this confusion within the Christian community if what you have just shared with me is true and as simple as you make it out to be."

"You open up a lot of areas to talk about," I respond, "but I'd like to first address why I think there is so much confusion among the people who label themselves Christian, yet have so many disagreements amongst themselves. This was a puzzle for me for a long time and kept me away from Christianity, but now I believe I have an explanation that works."

"Let's hear it."

"Okay, but if I get too long-winded or you have questions,

just stop me.

"The basics of the Christian faith are really quite clear. The differences seem to appear, primarily, in the way different groups of Christians choose to worship and serve the Lord.

"Jesus loves all people. He has a very clear and simple requirement for those who wish to be accepted into His Kingdom and, ultimately, into His Heaven. A person must believe that He is the Savior of the world and that believing in Him is the only way. His commandments are also clear and simple. First, love the Lord your God with all your heart, soul, and mind—and second, love your neighbor as yourself.

"Let me give you an illustration of diversity yet with unity. The country of Mexico is made up of 27 different states. In each state and, even within sections of states, there are different styles of food preparation. They are all Mexican. So when you and I sit in a Mexican food restaurant in the United States, which Mexican state is represented?"

"Are you waiting for me to answer?"

"Yes, what do you think?"

"I think it doesn't matter. It's whether I like the food or not."

"I agree. In the same way, there are many different styles of serving and worshiping Jesus. I don't try to sort out the styles. I just enjoy all the styles in varying degrees."

"So you think all the diversity doesn't matter?"

"I actually think all the diversity is good, and, really, how different are they? Let's get back to the Mexican food for a moment. Those who prepare Mexican food use pretty much the same ingredients with variations in the spices and quantities of the ingredients. Tamales in one state in Mexico are different from those in another state, but to someone from a different country, they would be described as being very much the same.

"Here's the interesting part, though. If a foreigner made

that point to one of the local persons in a particular state of Mexico, the local person would be able to describe the differences, elaborate on the reasons for the differences, and defend the local way of making tamales."

"So, you think it's about using different quantities of the same ingredients that make up all the different Christian church styles?" My son is catching on—sort of. "I thought the Bible was very clear and specific on its rules."

"The Bible is clear. The variations come from the ways people read and apply the Bible to their lives. They tend to emphasize different things. Christianity is not about its rules. It's about who God is. Once we get that straight, then we can begin to grow in a personal relationship with Him. That is the essence of Christianity. Once we know the real God and have begun to read His Word, we will grow in relationship with Him."

"You make it sound very simple; too simple."

"I can't possibly explain how millions of different people read the same words and come up with so many variations in how they serve and please God. I can say that they treat it as a menu and emphasize the parts that suit them. I believe that some ignore the parts they should emphasize, but I don't think my opinion matters. God is, above all, a completely loving Father. It's possible that He not only likes the variety but actually prefers it. Some churches are formal; some are casual. Some stress the rules of behavior, and some stress the loving nature of God."

"Isn't that still confusing? Which is the right way?"

"The right way is to acknowledge Jesus as the Son of the One True God and to love Him with all your heart and all your soul and all your mind—and to love others as you love yourself.

"I believe all the confusion surrounding the varieties of Christian churches is over emphasized. It is possible to live according to the Bible and still have variety. We can't possibly understand all there is to know about the Bible any more than we can expect everyone to apply it in the same way. The Lord loves His children, and He does not expect perfection from them. He made each individual unique, and He does not expect us all to act and think exactly alike. He came and served as the sacrifice, so we don't have to be perfect, because He knew we couldn't be. He came in human form, so He knows how difficult it is for us to live correctly. Parents do not expect perfection from their children and neither does God. He expects and desires our love and a personal relationship."

"Then why are there so many rules in the Bible?"

"The rules are in place for our good. God wants to help us avoid the consequences of doing the wrong things. The rules are for us, not Him. He wants to spare us the hardships we would bring on ourselves."

"Why do people resent having the rules?"

"Why don't children want to do what their parents tell them to do? It's the mystery of growing up. How many times do you hear people your age saying they wish they had listened to their parents?"

"Sure I hear it." My son gives me a smile.

"Of course, at the time, people are reluctant to admit what they're doing is wrong. They want to keep on doing it because it brings them pleasure."

"I get it," my son quickly volunteers. "They want to see if this time it can be right and not wrong? They are pushing the boundaries out a bit further."

"I think you've got it. We should call that rebellion, don't you think? What do you think should be done when people rebel?"

"Well, there should be a consequence."

"There usually is. The consequence is almost always far greater than the discipline of the parents. This could go on and on, but I'd like to summarize. Okay with you?"

"Sure."

"There are many do's and don'ts in the Bible. They are all for our good. This becomes clearer as we get to know Jesus better. I think all new Christians should spend their first year or two just reading the Gospels (the first four books of the New Testament) so they'll get to know Jesus and understand His heart and His character. I think some confusion exists with other parts of the Bible because those things are not taken in the context of what Jesus is really like."

"So, for you it's all about Jesus."

"Yes, it's all about Jesus. It's about who He is, why He came, what He did, what He taught, and what He is doing right now."

"So, Dad, I'm not clear how people decide what style they will choose when it comes to serving and worshiping God."

"Most people don't consciously choose. They are born into a family that is Baptist, Methodist, Presbyterian, Assembly of God, etc. As children, they become familiar with a certain style of worship and service. Others may go to a particular church because they are invited by their friends or extended family. People don't usually begin by studying the Bible and choosing a church based on the way they interpret what they read. Many don't even realize there are differences. That's not really so important, is it? As long as people love Jesus and are building a personal relationship with Him, the type of church they choose is secondary. It's a decision each person has to make for himself.

"In my opinion, it might even be healthy for people to change churches a few times. Their spiritual needs may change as they raise their families, grow older, or move to another location—you know, different stages of life."

"What do you mean by 'different stages'?"

"At times people move to a church because it has a better program for children, or the teaching from the pulpit is more positive, or the teaching is more history focused or more socially relevant, or it seems more like the church they attended as a child. Some people in a formal worship environment may want to try something more casual or the other way around. We all go through stages in our lives where we have unique needs."

"Are you saying every church is okay?"

"No, I'm *not* saying every church is okay. I'm saying that any church that believes that Jesus is the Son of the One True God, studies and teaches only from the Christian Bible, and believes Jesus is the only way to God is, very likely, an okay church. The social aspects, teaching, or worship styles of the church are not important."

"You seem to be so accepting of all churches; how will I know when one is wrong?"

"That's a good question and one I'm eager to answer. I would not attend a church—even if it calls itself 'Christian'—if it does any of the following:

1. Takes its primary teaching from any book other than the Bible.
2. Expresses a need to control the details in the lives of its members. Control by others, even religious leaders, is wrong and not a part of the Bible. A Christian's relationship with God is supposed to be direct—Jesus is the only mediator.
3. Emphasizes one or two rules or concepts in the Bible without putting them in the context of the complete teachings of Jesus. Jesus is the final authority sent by God to tell us and show us what we are to think, feel, and do.
4. Fails to present a pervasive sense of mercy and gentleness and caring and love.
5. Teaches concepts and ideas that are not supported by Scripture.

6. Fails to teach the principles of the Bible in a way that rightly represents the character and nature of Jesus, as presented clearly and simply in the first four books of the New Testament."

"You mean there are churches that do these things?" my son asks in amazement.

"Yes, there are, and they are sincere and, yet, sincerely *wrong*. People need to read and study the Bible so they'll realize when a church is not rightly representing God or the Bible."

"So, Dad, you don't think having all these varieties of churches is confusing?"

"The confusion subsides as we recognize that varying styles of worship and service can be an advantage for the Christian church. People are free to find a good church where they are comfortable in their preferred style. God, The Father, is the best father in the world. He has many children who, for many reasons, have very different tastes and preferences. He gives those children free will to make their choices. He is the 'Great Encourager' of all this variety."

"What about religions that are not Christian?"

Other Religions

I take a deep breath and move forward.

"Any time I talk about other religions being 'wrong', I want to make sure you know that I'm not talking about the people being 'wrong'. I'm referring to their beliefs. Most people get their belief system from their families. If I had been born in another country without the opportunity to study as I've done, I'd probably be a devoted follower of the religion my parents espoused. I make no judgments about individual people."

"Dad, aren't you being a bit wishy-washy? Don't you have a firm belief?"

"I am eager to make a firm stand on what I believe, but I'm just as eager not to condemn other people. In my study of other religions, I begin with understanding the person who is credited with starting it, and then I focus on the book or books they use to promote their beliefs."

"Do you think people in these other religions will go to heaven?"

"I know it's my responsibility to do everything possible for them to hear the Truth."

"You're being evasive."

"As I read God's words in the Bible, I'm left with a clear understanding that people who do not come into a relationship with God through His Son, Jesus, will spend their eternity in a very bad circumstance."

"Why are you so apologetic?"

"I'm not apologetic; I'm concerned. Imagine people who have been loyal and obedient to their families for generations who will not be in heaven with Jesus. That makes me very sad."

My son sees the tears coming to my eyes and looks down. He isn't used to seeing me express my emotions in a public place. After I regain my composure, I continue to make the point.

"When I talk about other religions it makes me sad."

"Why? Shouldn't you be angry at them?"

"I can't be angry at them. I'm sad for them. They've been misled. I am angry with the one who deceived them."

"Who is that?"

"Well, this statement will probably make you feel uncomfortable, but I believe the source of all this is Satan—the devil."

"So, you believe in the existence of the devil?"

"Yes, I do. It doesn't take a lot of searching to find references to Satan in the Bible. I believe he's alive and active and busy working to lead people astray. The sad part is that he is very successful."

"So, people do wrong things because of Satan?"

"He is the source of all evil. He is the one who tempted Eve, which led to Adam's fall. He is the one who encourages, promotes, and supports all the evil in the world."

"Aren't people responsible for their own actions?"

"Yes, of course they are. But the devil knows how to use their natural tendencies to encourage them to be at their worst. I'm certain he has assigned specific demons, who work for him, to distract and lead people into wrong behaviors using their own wrong tendencies. These demons have thousands of years of experience to call upon to deceive people. I believe people are at a disadvantage if they don't know this is occurring."

"You seem very sure of this. Do other people believe it?"

"Yes, there are millions of others who believe as I do. They are the ones who read and believe what the Bible says, and they don't try to hide from this reality. The Bible is filled with examples of this happening and there is an abundance of real examples occurring today.

"There are many things to say about this, but I'd like to hold it for later and get back to the topic of other religions. Basically, here is the point. I believe the devil is behind all these incorrect religions. The timeline of the history of religions since 2500 B.C. until today (4500 years) is a schedule that includes the creation of many false religions. We can track how the devil has used religion as a means to keep people from knowing and understanding the One True God. I can show you with a few examples what I mean and then, if you feel its necessary, you can do additional research."

"Why is this so important to you?", my son asks. "I can tell by your intensity that this is an important point for you."

"It is one of the most important points I'm going to make today. The devil is alive and active. He hates all of us more than you can imagine. If people knew this, they would understand more of the confusing things that go on in their lives and the lives of those they love and want to help. Imagine an intrusive and deceitful spiritual being whispering 'wrong' things into your mind—and it seems like it's coming from inside you. I'm not talking just about the dramatic and awful things you see in movies, but things like anger, lust, and gossip that cause or encourage us to think and say things we later wish we hadn't and knew we shouldn't."

"What about the things we see in movies? Is that real for people to hear voices and then do the terrible things they are told to do by those voices in their heads?"

"Yes, it's real, and even non-Christian psychiatrists who work with these people say they really do hear voices. It's very real to the afflicted people, but, let's get back to the other religions, okay?"

"Yes, I'm ready to hear how the devil is behind all these other religions."

"In the Bible, Jesus calls the devil a liar and the father of lies. That's a strong statement from the source of Truth. I believe what Jesus says. That's my reality. I'm going to talk for a bit about a few religions, and you'll see how the devil worked to get them started."

I pause and begin looking through the materials in my briefcase.

"Is it hard to decide where to start?"

"Well, I have taught on this topic a few times over the past years. I thought it would be good to have my notes so I can be as specific and correct as possible."

I get my notes together and look up at my son.

With a big smile on his face, he says, "Are you ready? Should I give you a drum roll?"

We both laugh.

"Tell me about your teaching."

"The title is One God, One Truth. I talk about many of the things we're talking about today."

"Who is it for?"

"It's for church groups. The purpose is to encourage believers and let them know that their Bible is like no other book so they can trust what they are taught from it. The hope is they will be better able to explain to other people, in a logical way, what they believe, and do it in a way that is clear and simple. I'm careful to present the hard facts but not in an offensive manner. I believe it's easier to be firm in an opinion without being argumentative if we are sure about our points and the foundations upon which we base those points. A key goal is to help get rid of many of the reasons for doubts some believers may encounter in their private and personal moments. I don't want them to have any doubts. It's designed to give them additional information they can use to establish their firm foundation."

"Sounds like you enjoy doing the teaching."

"I do very much."

I flipped through my notes until I found the right page.

"Let me talk about how the Muslim religion, Islam, was started. The source for much of this is in a book entitled *Handbook of Today's Religions* by Josh McDowell and Don Stewart. They did a great deal of research and quote the work of other writers extensively. I'll give a brief history of the religion and the man who started it.

"A man named Muhammad was born around 570 A.D. in Mecca, a city in Arabia. His parents died when he was young, so his uncle raised him. At the age of 25, he married a wealthy 40-year-old widow.

"Muhammad was a very unusual man who was said to have 'fits' in his younger years. He told others he thought he was demon possessed. By the time he was 40 years of age, he had become religious and believed there was only one God, Allah. He had visions and received messages he believed were from God. When he shared these messages, visions, and opinions, his followers would memorize them and, eventually, they wrote them down. These writings were compiled and became what is known as the Qur'an—the most holy book for Muslims. Muhammad was the only source and he is credited with being the primary, if not sole, writer of the Qur'an. He called himself the one true prophet of Allah."

"So, the only source for information about Allah is through the writings of Muhammad in the Qur'an?"

"The Qur'an is certainly the primary source and Muhammad is considered the one true prophet."

"How long did it take him to write the book?"

"His followers recorded his sayings from the time he was forty until he died at the age of 62."

"What was he like as a person?"

"Clearly he was very bright and a great leader. People began to follow him, and he must have been a powerful speaker and leader because he had many committed followers. His style of writing would cause some to think he was more like a poet than a religious scholar.

"The religious leaders in Mecca believed in many gods—approximately 360 represented by different physical items such as rocks or carvings were housed in a central building. Understandably, Muhammad's strong opinion that there was only one god whose name was Allah did not set well with them. He and his followers were forced to leave Mecca when he was 52 years old.

"Settling in Medina, Muhammad took control of the city and killed many people who disagreed with his religious beliefs. He continued to grow in power and build his army. When he was 60, he went back to Mecca and took it by force. His reputation as a brutal warlord is the least of the complaints about him. He was also a rapist and had many wives."

"If he was the brutal leader of an army that fought against his own people, doesn't that make him a traitor?"

"Muhammad believed he was doing what Allah wanted him to do. The government supported and condoned people believing in many gods and he was convinced that was wrong. Muhammad was not a traitor to Allah, but rather a messenger who believed he was required to spread the word of Allah even if it meant fighting and killing people.

"After his rise to power, the rest of the Arab world rallied around him, and he unified the area for the first time. He was a great and very successful political leader. The Muslims of today still follow him, although they also have

their own styles of what they do and think is important—
just like Christians. We hear on the news from Iraq and Iran
that there are many factions even within cities and villages.
It seems to be universally true that people have trouble
agreeing on the details!"

My son gives me a big grin.

"Did Muhammad know about Jesus?"

"Yes, he did, and he believed Jesus was a great prophet,
but he thought himself to be greater."

"Muhammad thought he was greater than Jesus?"

"Yes, Muhammad came along 550 or so years after Jesus
and there were many Christians in Mecca. Nevertheless, he
did not believe that Jesus died on the cross, rose from the
dead, or that He was the Son of God. He believed Allah was
the one and only god and that he did not have a son—
Muhammad believed he was his last and greatest prophet. He
believed the writings of the New Testament had been
distorted and changed."

"Why would he believe that?"

"He had been receiving revelations from dreams and
visions and visitations by an angel who called himself
Gabriel. By the way, that is the name of the angel who
visited Mary, the mother of Jesus, to tell her about the
coming baby Jesus. However, it is clearly not the same angel.
It was in these dreams and revelations that Muhammad
received the information he spoke and his followers memo-
rized and wrote down. Also, communications were not the
same as they are today, so he did not have the benefit of
sending an email or doing an Internet search to check the
accuracy of his information.

"It is now clear that the New Testament was and is accurate, and it has not been changed or distorted. He was wrong.
That's a big flaw that makes it difficult to accept what the
Qur'an has to say as truth. It is well written and contains
many true statements. But it's impossible to believe that the

Qur'an actually contains the words of God. One man, with a questionable reputation communicated his views from his own perspective. Islam came from the views of a deceived messenger and an erroneous premise that other established documents were false—which they weren't.

"Where are the books written by many authors over hundreds of years foretelling the coming of Muhammad or someone like him? They don't exist. Where are the reports of Muhammad touching people and healing them from their physical and mental illnesses? Where are the reports from eyewitnesses confirming he was alive after his death? Where are the reports that he showed great compassion to many people? Where does it say that Muhammad claims he is God? They don't exist. Compared with Jesus, he ranks as far behind as any other human being. Apart from the Qur'an, he is credited with murder, rape, child molestation, and many other evil acts. It is easy for me to dismiss Muhammad, the Qur'an, and Allah without any additional information, but there is more."

"Then why do people believe in Allah and Muhammad?"

"They don't have the information about Jesus that we have. They don't have any information to refute the teachings of Muhammad. If they did speak out against Muhammad, they would run the risk of being killed. Do you need to hear more or is that enough?"

"Yes and no. It would be okay to stop with these answers, but I'm eager to read more so I can understand it fully."

"I'm very happy you're going to do that. You'll have fun and learn many things that will, in the end, strengthen your faith in Jesus."

"Even though I'm going to do more reading, please answer a few questions for me. How is the God of Christianity different from Allah, the god of the Muslims?"

"The God of Christianity is the God who created the earth and left all the evidence with His chosen people, the

Jews. He is the God who sent His Son to show us what He is like. There were many eyewitnesses who testified that God's Son, Jesus, performed miracles and, after being crucified, rose from the dead and met with His followers. We learn about Allah, the god of the Muslims, through his prophet Muhammad—the only source of information in all recorded history. That's not enough for me.

"On the other hand, the New Testament was written by nine or ten people, who are all in agreement concerning the nature and character of God and Jesus. The Old Testament was written by 35 or 40 people over a 1400-year period and many of them foretold events that occurred in the recorded life of Jesus. The evidence is very much in favor of the God of Christianity."

"So, with the Bible, we have more writers over a longer period coming into an amazing agreement and prophecies that were literally fulfilled. With the Qur'an, there is one person writing his opinions and editorializing about things—like saying the Bible is not accurate, when it is."

"That's a succinct summary."

"Dad, is the description of Allah similar to the description of the God of Christianity?"

"There are similarities in terms of them being all powerful and the creator of all things, but they are very different in terms of how they relate to people. Allah is said to be far above and uninvolved with individuals. The God of Christianity knows each of us personally and is involved with the details of our lives. His Son, Jesus, taught that God, the Father, knows about every bird, as well as the number of hairs on each of our heads. Jesus is eager to work in the lives of individuals through the Holy Spirit to make their time on earth better. The Bible tells us that Jesus is at the right hand of God, the Father, where He is the advocate for each person who believes in Him.

"The teachings about Allah are that no person is worthy

of getting into heaven, and Allah alone decides who does and who does not end up there. The requirements to get there are not clear. Allah has the right to be arbitrary and inconsistent in deciding who he lets into heaven. There is another confusing element—it isn't really clear, but it seems to be saying that a person can be guaranteed entry into heaven if he or she has killed an infidel. Getting into the Christian heaven is clear and simple—you must simply believe that Jesus is the foretold Messiah and worship Him only."

"What about this killing an infidel business? What is an infidel?"

"An infidel in the Muslim religion is anyone who is not a Muslim, but Muhammad took special aim at Jews and Christians."

"Why is there such hatred for the Jews and Christians?"

"The complete answer is very lengthy. I can loan you some books to study on the subject. The short answer is that the heritage of the Jews and the Arabs is connected back to the time of Abraham. Abraham received a promise from God that he would have a son to be his heir. This was a key part of the beginning of Abraham's legacy. The promised son with Abraham's wife, Sarah, was slow in coming, so Sarah asked Abraham to have a son with her Egyptian maid, Hagar. Abraham did have a son with Hagar, and they named him Ishmael.

"Thirteen years later, Sarah had her first son (the son of God's promise) to Abraham. His name was Isaac. After Isaac's birth, trouble developed between the mothers, and Ishmael and Hagar were forced out. The God of Christianity (Jehovah) then promised Hagar that her son, Ishmael, would also be the father of many nations. He is recognized today as the father of the Arab nations. So ... the connection and the conflict go back a few thousand years."

"Why is there such hatred?"

"The hatred begins with the fact that both the Arabs and

the Jews each claim to be the rightful heirs of Abraham. The Arabs are the descendants of Ishmael and the Jews are the descendants of Isaac. It's a long-running feud that is fed by a complicated set of issues surrounding their history, beliefs, and real estate."

"This is an old story covering a long period. Is history clear on this and do both sides understand it?"

"Yes, the people who study know. Those who don't study accept the generally proposed truths they've been living with for years or even centuries. Most of the common knowledge is skewed to meet the needs of the people who are now in control of these areas. They are focused on preserving their power, and they manipulate everything to meet that objective."

"That means that many of the people who are in the conflict don't really understand the conflict."

"Right—they understand their side of the conflict, but they may not know enough to have a full understanding. When this happens, people tend to go along with the thinking and emotions of their families and friends."

I begin looking through my teaching materials.

After a minute or so, my son asks. "What are you thinking we should discuss next?"

"We need to talk about counterfeiting," I quickly reply.

"Counterfeiting?"

"I want to make a point about how people are deceived."

"What point?"

"If you want to deceive someone, consider creating a counterfeit—it's quite effective."

"I agree, but how does that apply to this discussion?"

"Remember earlier I told you that Jesus called the devil a liar and the father of lies?"

"Yes, I remember."

"Well … the devil is also very good at deceiving people by counterfeiting the truth. He makes it look almost the same—so close that some people can't tell the difference—and then he changes just a few key points. For example, if I wanted to counterfeit a dollar bill, I would not use red ink but an ink that's close to the real color so the casual observer would not even notice. I would want to match as closely as possible the same paper, ink, and approved printing plates. Keep this thought in mind as I talk about the next religion."

"What is the next religion to discuss?"

"I want to discuss The Church of Jesus Christ of Latter Day Saints."

"Mormons, right?"

"Yes, and they are a very successful counterfeit."

"Why do you call them a successful counterfeit?"

"They are, as a group, more disciplined than any people I know at living according to a Christian religious style. The people are extremely nice, very bright, very industrious, helpful to one another, and noted for abstaining from certain dietary items. They are very committed to regularly participating in the activities of their churches. They lead disciplined and admirable lives."

"Then what is the problem?"

"The problem exists with the founding father of their beliefs and the source of Mormon beliefs.

"In 1820, a young 15-year-old man by the name of Joseph Smith had a visitation from two 'personages in light,' which he understood to be angels. These creatures told him not to join any of the existing Christian churches in his hometown because they were not 'true' churches. He was instructed to wait patiently for their return, at which point they would tell him about the 'true' church. According to Smith's report, these 'personages in light' did return a few years later. They led him to a set of gold plates, which he said he was able to read through a special pair of large eyeglasses. The writing on the plates is the source of the *Book of Mormon*. They contained stories about an ancient people who lived in the Americas thousands of years ago."

"Did these people exist?"

"There is no archaeological or historical support for the existence of these ancient people or the places mentioned in the book. Some detractors have strong evidence that the *Book of Mormon* was plagiarized from romance novels about the American Indians written by a retired Christian preacher.

"Interestingly, nine people —all close friends or family members of Joseph Smith—actually signed a document stating that they had seen the original plates. They are the only witnesses. As far as we know, these plates do not exist today and no worthy explanation has been offered for their disappearance.

"Joseph Smith had a reputation for spending a lot of time digging for treasure using a 'peep stone' to locate where he should dig. His reputation was one of a treasure hunter who wanted to get rich with his discoveries."

"Did he get rich?"

"It's not clear that he ever got rich, but he did get the *Book of Mormon* written and he did get himself killed by the local people in Nauvoo, Illinois."

"Why and how did they kill him?"

"He had been jailed for vandalizing the local newspaper office that had reported negative things about his religion. One of the keys to the Mormon religion is polygamy and this issue was a problem for most of the people at that time. The locals took things into their own hands, stormed the jail, and killed him and his brother."

"He had an established church by this time, I guess?"

"You guess right. The church started in 1830 in Ohio, and then moved to Illinois. Joseph and his brother were killed in 1844."

"What happened?"

"The Mormons continued to be persecuted. Finally, Brigham Young, who became the Mormon leader after

Joseph Smith was killed, led a large portion of the believers to Utah."

"Why did he lead only a part of them to Utah?"

"Another man contested Young's authority. He and a few others refused to go along with Young's plans. The split in the church remains to this day."

"So, why do you consider the Mormons a counterfeit?"

"The problems are with their books, which are the sources of the church's teachings. The *Book of Mormon*, the *Pearl of Great Price*, and the *Doctrines and Covenants*—are all considered to be more authoritative than the Christian Bible. Their leader can make changes to the *Doctrines and Covenants* any time he wishes. Even the modern version of the *Book of Mormon* has received more than 3,000 edits since it was first published in 1830. The *Book of Mormon* is unstable and subject to change at the hands of men, while the Bible is not.

"Sometime in the '60s or '70s, the leader of the Mormons received what he called a revelation from God—'that it was now acceptable to allow dark-skinned people to join their Church.'"

"How did people in the Mormon Church react to that change?"

"They began recruiting people with dark skin."

"Was there a big resistance to this by Mormons?"

"Not much. These were nice people who were very obedient to their leaders."

"Okay, please continue."

"A big concern is that they say they accept the Christian Bible, but they seldom use it and always qualify it as being simply a holy book—not accurate from the original. They don't really use the Christian Bible as the only source of authoritative information. However, they were quick to use the name of Jesus in naming their church—even though they don't attribute to Jesus his full stature as the only Son of God and equal with God in their teachings.

"This is one of the reasons I call this a counterfeit. They use the name of Jesus, but their teachings are in opposition to the teachings of Jesus. They teach that Jesus is not any different than we are and that his spirit-brother was Lucifer, who became Satan or the devil. They also teach that God was once just like us. If we live properly, we can become like God—not only in His character but also in terms of power and control. Their teachings about God are very different than the picture painted by the Christian Bible. These are only a few of the differences between Mormons and Christians."

"Why have so many been fooled?"

"They aren't taught from the Bible so ... they don't learn about the Bible and its authority. The young Mormon missionaries who show up at private homes are very nice, sincere, and well prepared. In general, Mormons are known for clean living and doing good works. These are the visible things that attract people."

"Don't you think their clean living and good deeds will cause God to accept them into heaven?"

"I don't, and that makes me very sad. These are nice, well-disciplined people who have grown up in Mormon families or been recruited by their missionaries. They don't believe that Jesus is the Anointed One of God who came specifically in the flesh, as a man, to be crucified and raised to life and that believing this is the only way to get into heaven. They think their good works and good deeds will get them into heaven."

"I can hear in your voice that this makes you sad."

"Yes, it does. If I had been born into a Mormon household, or I didn't know the Bible and its authority, I could have been misled, as well."

"Is it hopeless for them?"

"As long as a person is alive, there is always hope. If

they will accept the Christian Bible as their sole authority and confess that Jesus is the only One in whom they must believe for their way into heaven, then they can be saved just like everyone else."

"Mormons have a very different understanding of who Jesus really is, don't they?"

"Yes, they do."

"Why did you jump from a discussion about Muslims to one about Mormonism, which was started here in the United States?"

"To make the point that they seem quite different on the surface, but they are similar in the way the devil uses them to deceive people. Consider these points:

1. Both leaders had visions and were visited by an angel or spiritual personages to let them know there was a different way than is presented in the Christian Bible.
2. The leaders had questionable personal backgrounds before, during, and after these visits.
3. The leaders each wrote their own book to replace the Bible.
4. The writing is attributed to only one person.
5. The leaders were noted for their need and desire to have many wives.
6. Their concepts of God are different than is in the Christian Bible and, although they are different from one another, the concepts fit the leader's personal style."

"What do you mean by their personal style?"

"Muhammad was raised in an environment where fathers were very distant and uninvolved with their children—that's how he described God. Joseph Smith was raised in a household where there were rewards for good discipline, and that's how he described God's basic viewpoint. They each created a concept of God to match their own comfort and needs.

"If we are to know the One True God, we must see Him as He is described in His own book—the Bible. One of the difficulties many Christians face in their relationship with God is to successfully overcome their bad experiences with authority. Often these bad experiences provide a barrier preventing them from getting to know the true nature of God; Jehovah, the God of Abraham, Isaac, and Jacob. I am emphasizing the specific identity of the God I'm talking about. He isn't one I've created to match my personal style. I'm talking about Him as He is and is revealed in His Bible—a book like no other book on earth."

"You said that both Muhammad and Smith reported they were 'visited' by angels. That seems odd to me. Were those real experiences or did they make them up?"

"In the Christian Bible, there are accounts of 'visitations' both by angels and by demonic beings. So there is biblical support for this being a very real experience for these two men. That's one of the reasons why they were so strongly committed to following through with what they were being led to do.

"Don't get me wrong—I don't believe the 'visitors' to Muhammad and Smith were from God. God would not contradict Himself by having them write books with teachings that conflicted with the Bible, which we already had. I believe these visitors were sent by Satan, the father of lies. And they've been able to deceive many people; specifically, the 1.2 billion Muslims and 10 million Mormons in the world today.

"Neither of these two men were firmly aware of the truth and accuracy of the Christian Bible. If they had been, the deceiver would not have been able to use them. One was eager to go to war and the other was eager to have people follow him into polygamy. War, power, and polygamy were the primary tendencies used by the evil one to encourage these two men to be proponents of his lies."

"You don't seem very angry with these two men. Are you?"

"No, I'm not angry with the men, I'm sad for them. If you could see the picture in my head of the agony they are presently, and will forever experience, there is no way I could be anything other than very sad. I am angry with the deceiver. He duped these two guys, and now he stands laughing while they suffer. He hates them, but he was delighted to use them."

"What can you do with your anger?"

"I can do everything in my power to tell as many people as possible about the truth in the Christian Bible and get them to follow Jesus. I can also encourage other believers to know and understand some of these facts so they will be more secure in their faith. Then they will be ready to explain to others why they know for certain they are on the right path. I can also encourage other believers to live lives that honor Jesus so that others will be drawn to Him. I can pray for wisdom, strength, and specific individuals to be drawn to Jesus. I can let people know that we are warned specifically in the Bible that Satan would come, as an 'angel of light', to deceive as he did in the case of these two men. After they were deceived, they were empowered by Satan to lead millions to their destruction. I can also let people know that, as Christians, we have the power to overcome Satan and his demons, but we must submit to God and call upon the Name of Jesus. We have nothing to fear."

"Sounds, like you have a plan."

"I have a mission and a plan. I pray to have love for others and zeal for their lives, as I know God has for them and me."

There is a long pause and we agree to take a break.

When we reconvene, my son opens with this question. "Dad, how come I never read or hear about the Chinese, India Indians or Japanese in the Christian Bible? I know that the Chinese have the longest recorded history, and yet they seem to be left out of the Bible."

"They have not been left out. Remember, from a historical perspective, the Bible covers the period from the creation until the first century A.D. The focus is on what some call the Middle East and parts of Europe. That is where the creation of man began and where God focused His early relationship with man."

"Yes, but why isn't the history of China and that area included in the Christian Bible. If God is the God of the whole world, why did He leave them out?"

"I'm sure they were not left out. Why are you concerned?"

"That area contains half the population of the world—yet they seem to have been overlooked. I wonder if that is why they created their own religions or do they really have another legitimate view of the God of creation."

"They have not been overlooked. God loves them and included them in His plans from the beginning. A book written by C.H. Kang and Ethel R. Nelson, *The Discovery of Genesis*, shows that the truths of Genesis, the first book of the Christian Bible, are found in the Chinese language. This is a very scholarly book, and it sets forth, very credibly, that the original Chinese people were part of the dispersion from the Tower of Babel, as described in the book of Genesis."

"How do they make this credible?"

"The research is detailed and well presented. It is not for a casual read, but I did clearly get from it that the language and the culture, as represented by their written characters, included many of the concepts and stories that are unique to the book of Genesis. One example is the use of three characters to form the word boat. The three characters represent:

1. A vessel to contain something such as water
2. The number 8
3. Mouths or people

"From this we can get that the word for 'boat' is made up of 8 people in a vessel, which summarizes the story of Noah.

"Another example is the three characters for 'dust' plus 'breath of mouth' plus 'alive' is the Chinese word for 'to talk'. Combine the characters for 'to talk' with the characters for 'walking' and you have the Chinese word for 'to create'. That sounds a lot like the teaching in Genesis about how God created man."

"Are there more examples in the book?"

"Yes, there are many more examples with a very substantial history of Chinese writing and how the courts of the various dynasties kept detailed records. They are able to demonstrate very convincingly that the Chinese were a monotheistic culture until around 500 B.C. when Confucius, Lao Tze, and Gautama showed up on the scene. Their One God was Shang Ti, who was Emperor Above All, and He created the heavens and the earth from a void. The information about Shang Ti parallels the information about Jehovah God as it is presented in Genesis."

"What changed their thinking?"

"That time—around 550 B.C.—was a time of wars and much social upheaval in China. Confucius was a man of humble beginnings who became a teacher and was well respected for his knowledge. He taught that people should behave like the people of times past when they were able to live together peacefully. This is considered the beginning of the Chinese reverence for the ancient ones—their forefathers. He was involved in local politics, but did nothing of particular note to distinguish himself or his career.

"After a weak political career, Confucius went to many

different areas and taught that people should seek the good of others. A book entitled *The Analects* contains the teachings of Confucius and his disciples. His followers continued his teachings and created a number of books, but this is considered to be the central one. His teachings focused on how the people should live together and presented principles for governing so the warlords would be kinder to people and all people would be kinder to one another."

"So, he did not claim to be a god or try to start a religion?"

"No. His followers turned his teachings into a religion after his death. He died in 479 B.C., but it took time before he was revered as a god. Around 1068 A.D., Confucius was raised to the level of Emperor even though he had been dead for more than 1,500 years. In 1906 he was officially recognized by the Chinese government as being equal with the deities Heaven and Earth."

"So, Confucius taught that focusing on social behavior patterned after the ancient people was the most important pursuit of man. How did this become a religion?"

"It became a religion because people needed something to believe in and his messages were very good. The worship of Confucius as a deity was conducted by the first President of the Chinese Republic in 1906. This may have had a political motive, but it served to show the people that the leaders accepted, condoned, and promoted the teachings of Confucius. They wanted people to know that being concerned about and seeking the good of others is the right way. They may also have felt it would cause people to be more compliant with their government. It was a very good political move."

"This is a very different view of God than we have in America."

"Yes, it is. It would be similar to us making one of our great political leaders or teachers a god long after their death because we liked how they talked about ways to improve our culture and, thus, our government."

"Now I'm curious about the other Eastern religions. What about Hinduism? Isn't that the primary religion of India?"

"Yes, Hinduism is the primary religion of India, but culturally they are very accepting of all religions. Hinduism has no specific individual founder. They teach that 'Brahman' is the impersonal Absolute from which all creatures and things emanate. No one can or is expected to grasp the full meaning of 'Brahman'. However, Brahman is three deities in one, with Brahma the Creator, Vishnu the Preserver, and Shiva the Destroyer. This is the closest a person can come to understanding Brahman. It is convenient though that the three parts create, preserve, and destroy are general issues impacting the world. In this environment, they are able to accept all manner of religious worship—from animals to inanimate objects to believing there is no God. This is quite confusing. The writings are beautiful, and they continue to add to them. Buddha came from this background."

"You mean Buddha was first a Hindu?"

"Yes, his childhood was spent in the Hindu teachings."

"How did he start his own religion?"

"He was born in 560 B.C. in northeastern India into a wealthy family and was protected in the early years of his life from seeing the terrible conditions of his countrymen. His name was Siddhartha Gautama. He did not get the name Buddha until he had progressed and became the Enlightened One. His father literally tried to keep him from going outside the grounds of their home. When he finally did go out as a man in his twenties and saw the agonies of life, he sat under a tree for seven days until he understood the truths of life. In summary, there are Four Noble Truths and an Eightfold Path."

"What are they?"

"It would take too long to present them properly in one

sitting. But I'll give you a quick summary if you promise to read about it in the next few days. The First Noble Truth is the existence of suffering. Not having what we want is suffering. The Second Noble Truth is the cause of suffering. This consists of having desires. The Third Noble Truth is the end of suffering. One must give up all desires. The Fourth Noble Truth leads to the end of suffering by the Eightfold Path. The Eightfold Path consists of the following steps: Right Views, Right Resolve, Right Speech, Right Behavior, Right Occupation, Right Effort, Right Contemplation, and Right Meditation."

"That sounds very hard to do."

"It is and so few people are successful at it that they believe they get many chances to do it again and again by being reincarnated. If one does not accomplish these truths and steps properly while they are alive, when they die they will be reborn in another form and get to try it all over again. If a person does succeed with the Eightfold Path, then he or she will reach Nirvana."

"What is Nirvana?"

"Nirvana is not easy to explain or understand even for Buddhists. However, it carries a meaning of a state of existence where a person has no desires. This state of attainment was attributed to Buddha, and he was credited as being the one to show the way. This is why his followers began to worship him."

"How can a person get to that state of thinking? I can't imagine even how to begin."

"That's what they teach. If it were easy, it wouldn't be as valuable."

"It sure is a lot easier to get to a satisfactory afterlife in Christianity. What is the promise of an afterlife for a Buddhist?"

"If a Buddhist reaches Nirvana by dying with no desires, he does not get reincarnated. Instead, that person becomes like a drop of rain in the ocean."

"They become a drop of rain in the ocean?"

"Well ... something equivalent to that. They become something that puts them in a peaceful place where they are at one with whatever is really out there in the unknowable."

"That doesn't seem very certain or exciting to me."

"I'd also like to point out that the teachings of Buddha are primarily from one man who was very bright, articulate, and led a good life. However, there were no books written foretelling his coming and then recording that he did exactly what it said he would do. He is similar to Jesus in that he was a respected teacher, but he was not able to do the things Jesus did. Buddha taught people how to live on earth and left the outcome up to them. Jesus taught people how to live on earth but also taught them how to get into Heaven. Jesus even said He would and did send a spiritual helper, the Holy Spirit, to be with us at all times to help us in this life. The Jesus way is much easier isn't it?"

"It is much easier, but I can see for some it might seem too easy."

"You're right. Many people are drawn to the foundational thinking that 'it's all up to me'. I guess the only way to get beyond that is to have a failure or two and get to the place where you recognize that you can't do it alone. Many people in America come to Christ during those times of crises."

"What about the people in other countries who don't have a Christian church down the street and a Christian friend within arms reach?"

"That's where missionaries step up to the plate and go to them. People by the millions in India, Russia, and China are accepting Jesus as their Savior. They are hearing the teaching and experiencing the power of the Holy Spirit through physical and emotional healings."

"Buddhists and Hindus are accepting Jesus?"

"Yes! Missionaries and evangelists are having the wonderful experience of seeing these peoples' lives transformed as they come to Jesus."

"Dad, sum it up for me. What have we been discussing for this past half hour?"

"The Eastern religions have the following characteristics:

1. Their supreme being is impersonal.
2. Their political/religious leaders were developed into gods after their deaths.
3. The teachings of their religions are focused on helping people endure the world with a weak potential for an afterlife.
4. If you don't do well in the current life you get another chance even though it may be in an even more difficult circumstance.
5. Each person is on his own to achieve his success.
6. The writings of their religious books are poetic, brilliant, and intellectually stimulating.
7. The culture, country, family, and religion are all woven together like an inseparable fabric."

"This is very different from Christianity."

"Yes, it is."

"What are the important differences when considering Hinduism and Buddhism?"

"One that comes to mind is that they are religions of ideas. By that I mean the ideas are first and people are second. Christianity starts with what God did and wants to do for people. Eastern religions begin without a clear statement of the nature of God and continue with what people are supposed to do to manipulate or live within a system they really can't grasp."

"What do you mean by 'manipulate'?"

"The teachings and the requirements are like a maze of emotional and intellectual twists and turns that don't have a clear potential for working out in a person's favor. For example, try to imagine how a person is going to get to a state of thinking in which he or she has no desires. It seems impossible except in a few rare, isolated, and extreme situations. In one sense, I admire the followers because I would be too discouraged to even begin. There isn't enough sense of hope for me. However, the teachings are very good regarding how people should behave toward one another."

"It seems to me you've talked more about the founders of these religions and the books they've written or used than you have about the various teachings. Did you do that for a reason?"

"Yes, my purpose was to focus on the source of the writings and the character and circumstances of the people who founded some of the religions. In a casual reading there are many similarities in the various teachings. All seem to address the issue that it's better to treat others well.

"The big differences center around the promise of an afterlife and what is required to get the best life after this one ends. In all considerations and comparisons, Christianity is far superior to all the others. Christianity's God is described as loving, merciful, and involved in the daily affairs of people. There is also current, significant evidence of an active and living God, exactly as described in the Christian Bible, working in the lives of people today."

"How does the evidence of Christianity match with the current findings in the world of science?"

Science versus Christianity

I open the conversation with an explanation. "Science is a friend of Christianity. Archaeology, the study of ancient documents, biology, physics, and history all provide significant support for the foundations and truths of Christianity."

"That's sure not the general consensus of most teachers in the colleges, universities or the leaders in the news rooms of our day."

"No, it isn't, but that should not be a surprise. In their eagerness to oppose Christianity, these leaders are required to ignore a lot of data and information that they should explore. Many seek out data points, pieces of information, and even speculation that they feel can support their established beliefs. I've often wondered why people are so ready to dismiss information that supports Christianity and so eager to accept information that is distorted or irrelevant."

"Why do they?"

"Accepting Christianity means admitting that they've done wrong and letting someone else rule and reign in their lives. That isn't very comfortable for most people. So they toss truth aside rather than admit their own failings. Some even feel they are providing needed balance to the majority of Americans (85 percent) who profess to be Christians.

"A significant part of the scientific community spends their time trying to understand how God made the things they are studying, so they can further their abilities to heal people, improve living standards, improve travel safety, and, in general, improve the lives of their fellow humans. I think this is a wonderful part of God's plan. Even when you consider how smart some of these researchers are, I don't think they would be successful if God did not enable them to succeed in their efforts. They can be inspired by God even if they are not currently one of His committed children. The Bible and history are filled with stories of rebellious people doing and accomplishing wonderful things for the benefit of others."

"Please give me examples of what you mean by 'understanding how God made things'."

"Consider, for instance, DNA. Scientists didn't create DNA—they 'discovered' it. We are all impressed by what they have done with the mapping and the promises this understanding implies for improving health care. It is mindboggling and wonderful. Let's remember though that DNA has been around since the beginning, and we are just now identifying it.

"Stop for a moment and consider that God created the complexity of DNA as a concept before He created man and installed it as a mechanism to build uniqueness into each person. He only has to use a fraction of each strand of DNA to produce significant differences in 12 billion people (the estimated number of people who have lived on the earth from its beginning). If we revere the people who discovered DNA, how much more should we revere the one who created the concept and implemented it long before Hippocrates lived or the microscope was invented? And remember, He did all that with dust, His breath, and His spoken words. That gives me goose bumps."

"I understand the awesomeness of the creation of DNA, but what else does it mean to you? I can sense you are going somewhere with this."

"Yes, I'm going somewhere all right. The God who created DNA loves me and billions of other people. Not only that, but He's eager to be involved in the details of our lives. If He can handle the details and complexity of DNA, surely I can trust Him to handle the details and complexity of my life."

My son stops, furrows his brow and speaks. "What does that mean?"

"It means I have a loving God, who is ready and eager to work and guide me through any of the issues I may have in my life. He loves me and I know it. When I'm going through tough times, He is using those things for my good or the good of someone else. The things going on in my life may be to teach me something I'm not doing properly or they may be opportunities for me to demonstrate my confidence and trust in Him—and that demonstration may be motivational or helpful to someone else. My tough times may also be an opportunity to prepare me to minister to and encourage others as they go through similar things. It is all about being helped and helping others so our characters will be shaped, and we can be more useful in God's Kingdom on earth. We won't be doing all this in heaven. Life on earth is just for a short while."

"You make it sound simple and easy. Is it really?"

"It is simple, but it's not always easy. It gets easier as you grow in your relationship with God through the power and help of the Holy Spirit. Part of maturing in any relationship is getting to know what to expect from the other person and then building comfort as expectations are met over time. You build confidence in a relationship when the expectations are met. God is eager to become our closest friend, if we do our part to seek and nurture the relationship. This is described in the Bible as a goal for the believer and a desire of God's heart for each of us—a unique condition if you compare it with the gods of other religions. Once people from a different religious heritage get to know about Jesus and His desire to be their friend, they will know that is very different than the god or gods of their family's religion."

"You do get a little carried away, don't you?"

"Yes, and I hope it doesn't put you off. I've had a hard time getting to these truths because the things of this world distracted me. I felt the whole religion thing was too complicated to be understood clearly. But after careful study, it is now very clear to me, and I want to share that clarity with everyone I can."

"No, Dad, it doesn't put me off."

"Good—because that's why I'm here sharing with you. I want to present all this to you in a way that is easily understood. I'd also like my life to reflect the impact of all the good that God can do in a person's life."

"Hey, I've got a question. What about the theory of evolution and Charles Darwin? How does that area of science stack up against Christianity?"

"Evolution does not disprove the existence of God. Darwin's theories began with the discovery that animals and plants change over time to adapt to their changing environment. That work is fairly sound and accepted by most everyone. The confusion came when Darwin took a huge leap and concluded that we all began from a common substance. That doesn't prove out. The data is clear that there are huge gaps in his progression of the timeline of man, as well as other animals and plants. New, clearly unrelated animals and plants appear that are not in a progression and cannot be confirmed to come from the same substance. Darwin and his followers do not explain these occurrences well."

"You don't seem to be very impressed with Darwin."

"I'm very impressed by his work as a biologist. I just

can't buy his conclusion that everything came from the same substance. All I can say is that those who entertain this theory as a possible truth really haven't taken enough time to look at the evidence. The case for creation as described in the Bible is much more credible. Our schools now feel they have to teach evolution as it has an accepted place in the history of science, but it is totally lacking in its ability to explain the creation of man.

"One of the reasons the theory of evolution persists is that it's a handy alternative explanation for those who want to reject God or at least put Him off. The interesting thing is that Barna Research—you can find them at www.barna.org if you would like documentation—states that 60 percent of adults in the U.S. agree that 'the Bible is totally accurate in all its teachings,' and 69 percent believe in God when described as the all-powerful, all-knowing, perfect creator of the universe who rules the world today.

"I mention those statistics because the media at large perpetuates the perception that only a few people believe in a living and all-powerful God as described in the Bible. The media at large also encourages the belief that most people accept the theory of evolution as a reasonable explanation for how man was created. These statistics prove that to be erroneous. This attempt to fool people with wrong conclusions from incomplete data has not worked."

"Is it true that Charles Darwin professed an acceptance of Jesus near the end of his life?"

"A book written in 1994 by James Moore, entitled *The Darwin Legend,* addresses that question in detail. It is based on thorough research and states that it's impossible to arrive at a firm conclusion on the matter. You need to read that book and then draw your own conclusions.

"One fact I found particularly fascinating in the book was that Charles Darwin came from a long line of active believers and only Darwin and his sons were skeptics or agnostics. Darwin's wife and daughters remained committed believers. I tell you this because it fits the pattern of a person rejecting God to further his own social standing with the group he desires to impress. It is fair to state he rejected God, because he was recognized as a believer for many years. The book by James Moore presents evidence that he may have resumed his relationship with Jesus, but it is not conclusive. If Darwin did want to resume his fellowship with God, it's my belief that he would have been welcomed with open arms, a big smile, and roars of cheering from the angels."

"Dad, you know I've been a fan of Star Wars and that type of entertainment for some time. Do you think there are other planets or universes out there with humans like us living in a similar environment?"

"I've also enjoyed those movies, but I don't have a definitive answer for you. It isn't a question I explore—but I don't have a problem with someone else exploring it. Their conclusions wouldn't alter the evidence and truths I live with today. No new information would alter my belief in God, His Son Jesus, and the Holy Spirit. I have all the information I need from the Bible, history, archaeology, science, and personal experiences. So, I enjoy the movies and view the implications of all the stories and interaction of the characters as being representative of the social and cultural complexities we have right here on earth.

"I'm also fascinated by the expanse and the beauty of the heavenly bodies presented in these movies. To me, they are a further demonstration of the mind and capabilities of God. We think we have mapped DNA, but we are a long way from mapping the expanse of the universe—or the universes we imagine, but haven't yet identified.

"One other thing that fascinates me is the rotation of all these heavenly bodies including earth. They are in continuous motion at incredible speeds. I can stick my head out a window of a car going 30 miles per hour and my hair blows flat on my head. I can stand in a park on a still day and my hair will not move—yet this earth is spinning around at 1,000 miles per hour. And, the earth is rotating around the sun at a speed of 67,000 miles per hour while it is spinning like a top at 1,000 miles per hour. That's incredible. No way can I fully understand that, but I can visually imagine it in my head. I know physicists can explain how that occurs, but they can't explain how it came into existence. I don't mean to minimize the work of physicists. I have a little understanding of what they do, and I respect them immensely."

"Speaking of physicists, Dad, have you heard of Stephen Wolfram and the book he published in 2002 entitled *A New Kind of Science?*"

"I have heard and read about him. Why do you ask?"

"He is talked about as the greatest new physicist to appear in a long time. What is his take on the universe and how man appeared on the scene?"

"I have a copy of his new book in my library. And even though I can't understand his message fully, I do appreciate its implications. He is a former child prodigy and, without doubt, a genius. What he produced and wrote about between the ages of 14 and 18 is much more than most physicists accomplish in a lifetime. I admire the ability of physicists to work so comfortably in the world of mathematical abstracts, which they turn into meaningful and useful information used by all branches of science. I appreciate very much what they do even if I'm incapable of understanding it completely.

"Wolfram's work revolves around an area of mathematics called 'cellular automata.' He explains his work with the help of one-inch black and white tiles. Starting with one tile and a fixed set of rules, a pattern is created. The example used by a writer who helped Wolfram with introductory public relations work as he launched his new science, was one in which one inch, black and white tiles 'grew' according to preset rules, resulting in a tile work the size of a football field that depicts a perfect black and white rose with all its detail. Wolfram contends this understanding will be the basis upon which all sciences will depend in the next few years.

"In an article in Forbes ASAP magazine, November 27, 2000, Wolfram is quoted as saying about his rule 30: 'It took me several years to absorb how important this was. But in the end, I realized that this one picture contains the clue to what's perhaps the most long-standing mystery in all of science: where in the end, the complexity of the natural world comes from.'

"Later in the article, Wolfram is quoted as saying, 'I've come to believe that natural selection is not all that important'. In this one statement, he dumps Darwin's conclusions as inadequate. He also says in the article that there is no room for God in his new science.

"It's my feeling that Wolfram has opened up an entirely new way of mapping the complexity of the universe. He has a unique and complex twist to explain how it works. But to jump to a conclusion that God did not initiate it is an incredible leap. He chooses to reject God rather than see his findings in the light of further understanding God's creation.

"I ask that you consider what Mr. Chaitin, an IBM research scientist, says about his friend Wolfram: 'Stephen is an exceptional man, and to his credit he's trying to do something revolutionary. He's trying to uncover the building blocks with which God decided to build the universe.' Even Wolfram's close friend admits that God exists. In the end, Wolfram's conclusions will not definitively dismiss the existence or work of God. Oh sure, some people will use his work to support their conclusion that God doesn't exist, but that kind of unfounded speculation has been going on forever, and it will almost certainly continue. It does not challenge or diminish what I believe. The more I understand their work and the extent to which these people are 'guessing and speculating,' the more I am reminded of how awesome my God really is. His power and mind are far above all I can imagine."

"Dad, I'm pleased you've read about Wolfram and his work. How did it come to your attention?"

"I'm always eager to read about new theories that attempt to challenge the existence of God. I wasn't a regular reader of that magazine at that time, so I believe the Holy Spirit brought it to my attention—perhaps just so I could share it with you and others. God doesn't want Christians to hide from science. I know that all I learn will reinforce my belief and expand my understanding of God. This is another example. Even the things in the Star Wars movies helped give me a better appreciation for the expansiveness of the galaxy and the God who created it."

My son nods and asks, "So, you believe the scientific community is made up of talented people who are 'taking apart' what God built so we can all benefit from the new findings and understanding they provide. Is that correct?"

"Sure."

"I majored in agronomy in undergraduate school. That is the agricultural science of plants and soil. It includes learning to understand the biology of plants, soil, and the interaction of water with nutrients in chemical reactions and processes to make plants grow. It is a fascinating field, essential to scientists who wish to 'take things apart' and 'put things back together in new ways.' For example, this allows farmers to use new breeds of plants, chemicals, and processes to grow more and better fruits, vegetables, and feed for animals.

"It is also a very good thing that all branches of science are continuing to 'take apart' and 'put back together' all sorts of things to improve our lives. I'm excited when scientists design or discover new things.

"In all scientific work, scientists start with and use what already exists in the world. They will never create something out of nothing—only God can do that. For example, a number of new elements have been added since I took organic chemistry. These elements have always existed, but only in recent years have they been isolated and identified.

"Wolfram may have discovered a new way to describe how some of the physics of the world works. Darwin may have discovered a new way to describe how some of the biological processes of the world work. But neither of them discovered anything that refutes the history, archaeology, and prophecies fulfilled in the Bible.

"The evidence of corroborating science, history, and archaeology confirms, without a need to speculate, the following:

1. There is a planet that exists, spins, and supports the life of animals and plants.
2. There is a place on the planet called Israel with a well-documented history.
3. There is a person of history confirmed by many witnesses, named Jesus, who was born, lived, died, and rose from the dead.

"While Jesus was living, He taught principles that enhance the social and moral lives of man. He also taught principles that give us insight into and familiarity with the supernatural world. He demonstrated His ability to do miracles, heal people, and raise people from the dead. He said He is God and that He is preparing a spectacular place for us—a place we can come to as soon as we finish our life on the earth.

"If I accept and promote the theories of Wolfram or Darwin, what do they offer as a reward after I cease to live on the earth? They make no offer—they don't even address the issue. They don't care about you and me. They simply want us to believe what they say so we'll demonstrate we think they are smart.

"If a person uses the theories of Darwin to further the study of biology—that's as it should be. If a person uses the theories of Wolfram to further the study of any science— that's as it should be. But to take their work as a basis to explain creation or the initiation of creation and then reject God is folly.

"If a scientist, who has rejected God, wants to debate this in scientific terms, a Christian scientist would be more than capable of responding. As a believer, I don't have to understand all things. Non-believers do not understand all things either. I do have to know, as a believer, that there is plenty of support for the Christian point of view. I can feel very comfortable dismissing wild conclusions and trust what I know from the Bible.

"The media and actions of the educational community could lead a person to believe that most scientists agree with their position about the need to teach evolution in schools. That is not true. It has taken only a few scientists, educators, and judges to promote and impose their minority position. Many of those participating in a decision-making role aren't qualified to evaluate the 'scientific' evidence any better than the rest of us. They simply have a position of authority.

"I believe many of them are not especially concerned whether 'science' is right or wrong. Many of them are just opposed to Christianity. They have rejected God. My hope is that these people will have their hearts and minds opened to embrace their Creator.

"I feel that some of these people may have had bad experiences with Christians and those incidents have caused them to reject Christianity without fully exploring its evidence and implications. I mention this to point out that every time we do a bad job of representing Jesus, we can potentially create an enemy for Jesus. The opportunity to engage the minds of non-believers with the Truth begins with engaging their hearts through right behavior, attitudes, and motives."

God is Alive and Active

My son's next question comes quickly on the heels of the last. "Is God really alive and involved in the lives of people today?"

"The answer is emphatically yes. And it should be possible to observe the evidence of this in the lives of Christians—those who have felt His touch and experienced His love and grace. Unfortunately, that doesn't always happen."

"Why not?"

"Wow, I don't know how to answer that question simply. It will take a while, and I may wander from time to time. Let me make a few points before we begin to sort it out.

"Many Christians go through their days seldom acknowledging the existence and presence of God. They focus on Him on Sunday at church, but they don't involve Him in the details of their lives. If they aren't aware and acknowledge Him, then He doesn't get recognized for the things He does.

"What I mean to say is that someone who narrowly avoids an auto accident may acknowledge the role of God in saving his life. A person who finds himself in a frightening or dangerous situation may call out to God to save him. But

for the most part, people acknowledge God for His interven-
tion in the big things. They seem to forget about the rest. So
… you may ask someone if they believe that God is alive
and active and hear them say 'yes'. But if you ask that same
person how actively involved God is in the details of his
everyday life, you would probably hear 'not much'.

"Here's another point to note. There are many dramatic
events occurring in people's lives today, including physical
and emotional healing—even miracles. Instead of applaud-
ing these events and thanking God for them, many Christians respond with suspicion, some even denounce them as
coming from a source other than God.

"Those who denounce the working of miracles do so
without a single legitimate item in scripture to support their
claims. Primarily their argument is that miracles and healings ended with the death of the apostles. There is nothing
in the Bible to support that opinion. It is precariously based
on their own personal experiences or lack thereof rather
than the Word of God.

"Of course there have been some counterfeit miracles.
(Remember what we've said about counterfeits?). And there
have been some who have used miraculous events to present
themselves in a showy or unusual manner. But to use these
intruders and exceptions as an excuse to dismiss all miracles
and healings is preposterous. The Bible tells us that this is
one of the ways the Holy Spirit works on our behalf and
these truths are demonstrated in the teachings and ministry
of Jesus. There are healings occurring today exactly as they
happened when Jesus was on the earth.

"Jack Deere, a pastor and teacher, has written a book
entitled, *Surprised by the Power of the Holy Spirit.* In this
book, he describes how God heals and works in the lives of
people today. He began his career as one who denounced the
miracle-working power of the Holy Spirit in the lives of
Christians today. After further study, however, he discovered

that nothing in the Bible supports the opinion that miracles and healings that come through the power of the Holy Spirit should not be occurring today. After he came to that conclusion intellectually, the Holy Spirit began to show him the reality of God's activities in the lives of people today.

"I had a similar experience. I had been reading and studying the Bible for more than ten years when I began to explore the role of the Holy Spirit. The teaching I was receiving at that time mentioned the Holy Spirit, but did not clearly define His role. I couldn't understand why He would be mentioned so often in the New Testament and sent by Jesus to help and encourage Christians, if He was not expected to be actively and vitally involved in our daily lives.

"I was taught to be suspicious of the miracles and healings, but I was hearing about them all over the world. The facts were in conflict with both the experiences I was reading about and the understanding I received from the Bible. That was cause for me to study it for myself and open up the possibility in my thinking that it could be true. As soon as I did, there were many incidents to support the reality of the active work of the Holy Spirit exactly as described in the Bible and specifically demonstrated by Jesus. I know the Holy Spirit is active and alive, because I now have personal experiences, in addition to God's Word, that demonstrate that truth. There is nothing to doubt. The confusion is gone.

"I apologize for getting so carried away, but it was a big deal for me to experience this new reality—even though I could see that it had been right in front of me the whole time, waiting for me to open up to it. I wish I had been taught about this many years ago. This active involvement of the Holy Spirit is available today even for all those who are suspicious or denounce it. It is authentic and very much in line with the events of the Bible. It is the teachings and work of Jesus."

"No, Dad, please don't apologize. This is good information, and I enjoy your enthusiasm. What about the healing shows on television? The people act a little 'unusual' and I wonder if they are real."

I posed the question. "Is it possible for people to be healed instantly of a physical ailment?"

"I'm now assuming it is because I hear so much about it, and you have assured me the Bible teaches it also. When I read about such events when I was younger, it seemed wonderful to me. It was part of what Jesus did, but not something I expected to happen in our time."

"That's what you were raised with, and your assumptions for today are correct. Instant healings occur in the Old Testament and the New Testament. So why do people have a hard time believing they are real?"

"One of the reasons may be that not all people who seek healings through prayer are healed."

"That is a very good point. For example, if there are 100 asking to be healed by the power of God at a specific event or time, only 5 or 10 or 20 may be healed. Many people focus on those not healed and question God's healing power. Others focus on those healed and rejoice in God's power being demonstrated. The facts remain the same. Some people are healed at that time. Some people are not healed at that time. The ones not healed do not cancel out those who are healed, but many dismiss it all by focusing on the ones not healed. I can't explain why all 100 are not healed. I can't explain why some reject the reality of the healings. I simply marvel at seeing those who are healed."

"I guess the point you are making is that healings are unusual even if they occur often and many people haven't experienced one personally. Also, it's clear to me that some Christians don't have full confidence in the Bible."

"That is correct and your point about lack of confidence in the Bible is another key to this."

"Yes."

"Why is it there are so many people certain there is a

city in France named Paris, and yet they've never been to Paris?"

"Well, it's on the maps, we see pictures on television, and it's shown in the movies."

"I have had more than one person tell me, firsthand, of personal healing experiences. I see people on television telling of their healing experiences. I read throughout the Bible that healings and miracles occurred. Jesus said it was one of the reasons He came. Jesus also said we would be able to pray and see it happen. It has continued to happen throughout the years since Jesus went to heaven. It will occur thousands of times today in almost every country in the world. Why won't people believe they're real? I'm wondering about the whereabouts of the doctors, experts, and media people who have proof they aren't real? These healings cannot be disproved because they are real. I submit that the thousands of healings daily are as real as the existence of the city of Paris in France."

"Then why do people reject it?"

"The people denying that healing is real have had no personal experience, and they avoid having those experiences. It is pure denial and an unwillingness to get the facts. Another point is that they would have to admit there is a spiritual dimension to our existence. Once a person acknowledges that, he finds himself opening up to a whole new way of looking at things. These people prefer to have their heads in the sand. The worst part of this is that people reject the One True God. They reject Christ. If someone rejects Christ, then they can also reject His healing. If they acknowledge His healing, then they have to undo their rejection of Him."

"What do you mean 'undo their rejection of Him'?"

"People have built a belief and acceptance system that rejects the truth of Jesus. To change this one belief would result in many changes and a rejection of much of who they think they are. One new piece of information causes them to have to reject the beliefs they have held for many years. I believe people are afraid to simply say 'yes', to acknowledge that instant physical healings through the power of the Holy Spirit are real and possible."

"Dad, I think I get it. First, they would have to admit they are wrong. Second, they would have to embrace the desire to change. Third, they would have to face and explain to all the people they've known for years why they are changing their minds. Fourth, they are afraid they'll have to change some of their habits and behaviors. I can see how this might be an overwhelming task to undertake. It is difficult."

"That's why there should be more mature believers working with new believers to help them overcome their fears and begin to believe God's Word. The changes would come easily if they had someone to help them. It is truly a big scary deal; however, the scary part goes away very quickly after a person gets started."

It is quiet while we both give thought to our conversation. It's an emotional time and mentally challenging. We're getting tired, but we can't stop. I begin again.

"My heart goes out to those who witness all this evidence and still reject Jesus. The fear in their minds is stirred up by the devil—the enemy of their souls. Christians need to pray for these people who are curious and exploring and be there to help them get through the transition. They need encouragement, a clear picture of what it will be like, and a lot of support as they make changes in their thinking. The devil is also alive and active and does everything he can to keep people from making a commitment to Jesus. So, we not only have our own natural tendencies and inclinations to keep us from committing to the Lord, but we also have to fight against the supernatural influence of the devil.

"People get uncomfortable when the devil is mentioned and a surprising percentage of people deny that he exists.

People want to believe that he is only a symbol of evil rather than a spiritual being who has a vast army to do his dirty work. The Bible is clear. He exists and he is actively involved in distracting and creating problems for people. Denying his existence does not make him go away. It leads to people being more vulnerable to his tactics, giving him more success."

"Even a conversation about him makes me uncomfortable, Dad."

"Yes, the thing that creates the fear and anxiety is that we feel inferior to him. However, by using the Name of Jesus we can have complete control over him and his minions. The power of Jesus' resurrection gives us that confidence, but we have to invoke the Name of Jesus. People who don't know Jesus are at a disadvantage."

"We've been talking about people who have not accepted Jesus. What about people who believe in Jesus, but don't believe He 'authorizes' instant healings today?"

"The issues and consequences are the same. They have to make the same difficult changes as the non-believer. In order to change, they have to reject and renounce all their years of speaking against healings and the workings of the Holy Spirit. Then they have to admit there is an alive and active devil who wants to make their daily relationship with Jesus less than it could be."

I pause and close my eyes. My son can tell I'm deep in thought and preparing to share the rest of my lecture. I speak.

"May I tell you why this makes me so sad?"

"Sure, go ahead."

I pause again for a few seconds, close my eyes, and rub my forehead and eyes with my left hand.

"Please let me rattle on for a while. I'm going to tell you a whole bunch of things. Feel free to stop me at any time, but I have a lot to say."

"Go ahead."

"I don't mean this to be critical, but I'm using it to describe an opportunity. Too many Christians don't know enough about Jesus. They know many Bible stories and important truths, but they don't know the purposes and character of Jesus as well as they should.

"I believe as soon as people come to accept Jesus and desire to know Him as their Lord and Savior, they should be guided to focus all their study in the first four books of the New Testament; the Gospels – the Good News. They should get to know Jesus through His teachings and by observing Him as He interacted with various people. Until they understand the heart of Jesus, they are likely to misunderstand the meanings and implications of the rest of the Bible.

"Too often people try to understand the teachings of the Bible before they understand the heart of Jesus. I know I'm repeating this point, but it's important so I wanted to say it two ways. Now I'm emphasizing it again.

"The reason I believe people don't properly understand the purposes and character of Jesus is that when I ask them why Jesus came to earth, they say to 'bring salvation to the world' or something like that. That is true, but it is not all we need to know.

"In the fourth chapter of Luke, we read that after Jesus had been baptized by John, He went out into the desert for forty days to be tempted by the devil. After this He came back to the city, went into a synagogue, and was handed the scroll of Isaiah to read out loud to those who were gathered.

"Jesus searched through the scroll (there were no chapters or verses in those days) until He came to a prophecy about the coming Savior of the world (our chapter 61). He read a small section aloud to the crowd. It went something like this; 'I have been anointed by God to preach the Gospel to the poor, heal the broken hearted, release the captives, free the prisoners, and proclaim the favorable day of the

Lord.' This is Jesus' mission. Salvation for the world was certainly His vision. His mission was the means by which He was going to accomplish His vision. It is clear and certainly concise, and all His teachings and actions in the Gospels are consistent with it.

"Jesus did not start from a high-up place in society. He preached to the average people. He comforted the down-trodden. He drove demons out of the mentally unstable to clear their minds. He healed the physically sick and lame. He raised the dead to walk again. He assured and demon-strated to people that His character was defined by love, mercy, grace, forgiveness, and humility, and He was eager to be close and personal with them. Wow! There is no other person in recorded history even remotely like Him. This is the central part of Christianity. It is about knowing Jesus; what He started out to do, what He did, and what He said, at the time He was going back to Heaven.

"What He said at the last was that His disciples should not do anything until they received the same power He had been using. When they received the power, then they would be witnesses for Him in Jerusalem, in the nearby cities, in the surrounding region, and throughout the world. He wants us to be witnesses.

"Witness is a noun. A witness for Jesus is someone who can speak with authority, lives in the truth and integrity of Jesus, and can attest to who He is. Near the time of His crucifixion, Jesus prepared His followers for His departure by telling them that when He was gone, He would send the Holy Spirit to give them power over demons and sicknesses, provide counsel, teach them, and live in them so they would be able to do all the things he had done.

"Today there are people who live in that promise. They pray for the sick, and the sick recover. They pray for those who are mentally and emotionally troubled and they return to their right and clear minds. The same things occur that

are recorded in the most accurate document of antiquity—
the Bible. This cannot be refuted.

"An airline ticket to Paris, France, is a few clicks away
on a computer and a six-to-ten-hour flight from wherever a
person might be in the United States. It is readily available.
A real experience of physical and mental healing is also
readily available for those who have a loving heart of mercy,
love, and caring. I pray that all people who reject Jesus or
His readily available power would be free to open their
minds and hearts to Him. He is real and the evidence is
everywhere and available to everyone."

"Dad, I'm sorry to interrupt."

"No, it's okay. I know I'm getting a bit passionate and
preachy."

"I want to get something clear in my mind. Are you
saying that the only thing standing between people and the
power of God is their fear of change or their stubbornness?"

"I think that's correct, and Christians who fully know
Jesus need to pray, exhibit Jesus-like character and behavior, and be available to these people. I do not mean to imply
they should badger people with their beliefs. I know love,
forgiveness, and deep concern for others will open doors of
opportunity for them to introduce people to Jesus and His
power."

Love and Forgiveness

"Dad," my son takes up a whole new theme. "I'd really like to hear some examples of God's love and forgiveness."

"Ah ... my favorite topic," I answer. "I'd be glad to oblige, and the place to begin is obvious. God loved us so much that He sent His Son to earth to die for our sins. He could have condemned us—thrown away His creation and begun again. Instead, He poured out His love and mercy on us. That's the greatest example of all.

"The second greatest example is the love and forgiveness Jesus poured out during His crucifixion. He asked His Father to forgive the men who were mocking, beating, and killing Him, even while they were carrying out their terrible acts. In the same way, He readily accepts and forgives us when we ask, no matter how long or for what reasons we have been rejecting Him.

"It's my belief that Jesus is eagerly waiting for those who reject Him today to change their minds. The Bible says He is standing continually at our heart's door knocking and waiting for us to invite Him to enter. Imagine it, Son—the God and Creator of the universe is 'asking' us to choose

Him for our own sake.

"And remember Peter, Jesus' disciple? He denied Jesus three times within the space of a few hours and at a time when Jesus most needed His friends to stand by Him. Even though Peter had seen Jesus heal people and walk on the water, he faltered and failed his Lord. Not only did Jesus forgive Peter, but He encouraged him and received him back into His service."

"That's amazing. Any other stories?"

"Wait! I can give you a notorious example from recent times. A certain young man was living an unspeakable life. He used men to gratify his sexual needs, and then murdered them. But that wasn't enough. This quiet, young man cut up the bodies of his victims, put them in his refrigerator, cooked, and ate them. Eventually, he was caught, convicted, and sent to prison, where another inmate killed him.

"The interesting thing is this. It was reported that while in prison, this young man accepted Jesus as his Savior. I don't know for certain if this is true—but let's assume that it is true. If this young man, who took so many lives in such a gross and unspeakable manner, did ask for God's mercy and forgiveness by accepting Jesus' sacrifice on the cross as payment for his sin, then I have no doubt he is in heaven right now. The Bible clearly teaches us that the gift of God's mercy and forgiveness is based on the pure and unblemished life of Jesus Christ, rather than our own corrupt and sin-ruined lives. Our God is incredibly forgiving and merciful.

"In the Bible there are stories of believers—strong believers—who went through times of doubt. Thomas and John the Baptist are examples. Jesus did not condone their doubts, but He did forgive them. I have entertained doubts myself. It's good to know I can ask for forgiveness and I will not be denied.

"I thought you were excited before, but now I see you were only warming up!"

"Well Son ... when you've experienced God's mercy and forgiveness in your life, you can't help getting excited about it!"

"Are there any other stories you could tell me?"

"Truthfully, there are so many stories that I could never tell them all, but let me tell you about a few more."

"I'm listening."

"The Bible tells the story of a woman caught in the act of adultery. It was the established law of the time to stone women caught in this situation. The crowd asked Jesus what they should do and waited to hear His answer. We are told that Jesus wrote something in the sand, something they all could read. Then he suggested that someone who had never sinned should throw the first stone. Of course by that standard, Jesus Himself was the only one qualified to condemn her, and yet He did not. Instead, He sent her home with the instruction to change her ways.

"Jesus' instruction to His disciples and to all Christians is to forgive seventy times seven. That is a figure of speech to let us know we are to forgive completely and as often as necessary. That is a reflection of God's heart and how He forgives.

"Christianity is often criticized because it is perceived as having a preoccupation with sin. But ultimately, Christianity is uniquely defined not by sin but by God's response to it—love and forgiveness. Those who accept Jesus as their Savior receive a complete and continuing forgiveness for all past, present, and future sins. Christians do not lose their assurance of salvation when they sin, but sin can temporarily separate them from fellowship with God. How wonderful to know that when we confess and repent of a sin, we are already forgiven. The confessing and repenting serves to restore us to an abiding fellowship with Him."

Seven and Six

We take a short break and then move on. "There are seven questions I would like us to explore", I tell my son. "The answers to these questions will help establish the truth and uniqueness of Christianity. You should also explore and be able to ask questions about other religions. I have a list of resources I will give you. The key is to be informed, rather than relying on self-developed opinions that get established through experiences or conversations with uninformed people.

"The seven questions are as follows:

"Question One: *Is the Bible accurate and complete?* The answer? Yes, it's accurate, and it contains everything you need to know about the Father, the Son, and the Holy Spirit. There are more than 24,000 copies and portions of New Testament documents used by experts to confirm the accuracy of the Bible. These copies date from 50 to 275 years after the documents were written. The existence of this number of copies and the short period of time after they were written are two statistics that establish the New Testament as the most accurate and corroborated document of antiquity. Also, the writers of the New Testament were eyewitnesses. Its authenticity is supported by history and archaeology. And we are told that we are not to add to the Bible, which would indicate that it is complete or at least all we need to know. We must judge everything in terms of it being in agreement with the Bible."

"Question Two: *Is Jesus a real person in history even apart from the Bible and did He fulfill the prophecies in the Old Testament about the coming of the Son of God?* Again—the answer is yes. Consider that even though Muhammad writes about Him incorrectly, he confirms that Jesus walked the earth. Many other historians confirm this, as well. He is an established person in history, and He did fulfill the prophecies in the Old Testament about the coming of the Son of God. Read through the first four books of the New Testament to confirm this. People who lived at the same time as Jesus and witnessed his actions and his followers wrote these books. Their accounts will confirm that Jesus did fulfill the prophecies."

"So ...", my son interrupts, "once you know that the Bible is accurate, you can use it as a complete and reliable source. Don't all believers know the Bible is an accurate source?"

"Apparently they don't. A research report by Barna Research indicates that 85 percent of Americans identify themselves as Christians, but only 44 percent of those Americans strongly agree that the Bible is totally accurate in all of its teachings. Earlier I told you 60 percent of adults in the U.S. agree that 'the Bible is totally accurate in all its teachings', now I'm narrowing that to the 44 percent who 'strongly' agree. This seems to be an opportunity for improvement."

"Why do you call it an opportunity for improvement and not an outrageous or unbelievable situation?"

"Many Christians are not as mature as they should be, and therefore, they don't get the full benefit of their relationship with God. They need more experience and knowledge in order to fully engage with our living and active God. This is where churches are equipped to help. In the same way that people go home to be nourished and fed, Christians should be going to church—their spiritual home—to be nourished and refreshed in their faith. Are you ready for question three?"

"You bet."

"Question Three: *Did Jesus perform miracles, heal the sick, and raise people from the dead?* The answer is yes. In addition to the New Testament, we have the writing of Josephus, the Jewish Historian, to confirm these actions in his writings.

"Question four: *Was Jesus crucified and did He die?*' The answer is yes. We have the writings of eyewitnesses as reported both in the Bible and non-biblical writings.

"Question five: *Did Jesus come back to life and did many people see Him?* Once again the answer is yes. There were hundreds of eyewitnesses. As far as I know no one from that time wrote convincingly that it did not happen. This was a big issue. If significant evidence existed, someone would have stepped forward to properly refute the fact that Jesus was raised from the dead.

"Question six: *Did Jesus have a positive impact on the lives of His followers?* Yes. His teachings encouraged them, convincing them that Jesus was the Son of God and that God loved them. His miracles healed people of physical and emotional illnesses. Many people were set free from personal torment and emotional problems. In the Bible we are told that Jesus raised a woman's only son from the dead, healed a woman with a serious blood disorder, and cured a boy who suffered from epilepsy. These people were all healed instantly.

"Question Seven: *Does Jesus have a positive impact on the lives of His followers today?* The answer is yes. His teachings encourage us today, just as they did when He walked here on earth. They help us believe that He is the Son of God and remind us that if we put our trust in Him, we can live a better life today and an incredible life for eternity. People, today, are being changed and healed emotionally and physically through the prayers of Christians. It is happening every day all across the world. The evidence is available in abundance. Our God is the Perfect Father who loves us and makes provision for us. Our God also allows us to make our own choices, and He designed the world so that choices result in consequences. This brings to mind our discussion earlier when we were talking about the eternal fire of hell. The Lord is loving and merciful, but in His perfect sense of justice, there has to be a consequence (hell) that is an exact opposite to the ultimate reward (heaven). As we contemplate one place, we can gain insight into the other."

I paused—waiting for a reaction from my son.

"So, what are you expecting to accomplish by focusing on these seven questions?"

"I want the basic points to be a foundation upon which people can begin their own exploration. I also want believers to know how to live with the answers to these questions so they will be encouraged and able to encourage others."

"Don't all believers know the answers to these questions anyway?"

"I'm not sure they do. I'm not sure they are equipped with ready answers so that if someone asks 'Why do you believe?' they can give a logical and reasoned explanation. I'm not sure they know what they believe or why they believe it. Given the current level of education and available information in the media, I would also recommend six considerations as people reason through their belief systems."

"Six considerations? What are those?"

"These are the six considerations:

"First Consideration: *There is no one else like Jesus and no religious book like the Bible.* There are no other religions with a leader like Jesus, whose life fulfilled many prophecies, who proved He is the Son of God by performing miracles, and who said He was the only way to heaven. I don't know of any other person even remotely like this. And there are no other religions with a book constructed like the Bible; containing the writing of many different writers—all in agreement—and detailing many fulfilled prophecies. These unique facts alone should help people dismiss consideration of all other religions."

"Second Consideration: *Science cannot dismiss the existence of God.* The works and writings of scientists who attempt to reject or dismiss God are best characterized as a maze of deception using sophisticated speculation. They take huge unsupported leaps in logic to draw their conclusions. Science is a discipline aimed at proving many things, and yet some of its most talented people have improperly skewed or ignored the facts in order to eliminate God from their theories of how the world was created. I can only conclude that they do it to rebel against God and simply further their personal sense of importance.

"For example, Darwin observed that certain animals had changed over time. The leap he took from that observation to the speculation that all creatures are descended from the same substance may have benefited his career, but, certainly drew him away from the principles of true science. Conversely, there are many respected scientists who have logical, deep, and extensive explanations to support the truth of creation as described in the Bible."

Once again I have become quick and animated in my speaking style.

My son laughs. "Tell me how you really feel, Dad."

I chuckle. "Well ..." I begin after a small pause. "I feel ... angry and sad and concerned and, at the same time, hopeful. I feel angry because the evolutionist side seems to be getting all the general media support, polluting peoples' minds. I feel angry because the decisions to change school curriculum policies are being made by a few judges. This should not be allowed. A minority thought by a minority group should not be imposed on the majority. I feel sad and concerned because too many people think the general media is properly informed and clearly they aren't. The impact of public media is too great at this time.

"I am hopeful, however, because I am aware of many efforts to make the Christian community better informed so they can begin to participate and actively influence the process. I am very optimistic that the truth will surface, but it will take a good bit of work."

"You sound optimistic. Are you really?"

"Yes, I am very optimistic. The information we have is strong and compelling. It needs to be presented properly, and then we have to get it out to the public in usable form. I'm eager to see the tide begin to turn in a few years."

"How many years will it take to see an impact?"

"I'm projecting that we'll see significant changes in awareness, beliefs, and attitudes in the next four to five years."

"That seems aggressively optimistic to me."

"I believe it's very attainable. The Internet, TV simulcasts, and sound teaching will all be used to move the cause along."

"Dad, what is the next consideration?"

"Third Consideration: *The discoveries of science cannot disprove the teachings of the Christian Bible?* Let's talk about three areas of science and study. History does not disprove the teachings of the Bible. Remember Josephus, the Jewish historian, who wrote in Israel in the very first years after Jesus' death, confirming Jesus' existence and His miracles. Nothing since that time has disproved it. I point out the absence of a document written by the Jews to disprove the resurrection—an event that influenced many of their own followers. The incident of Jesus' resurrection caused a major stir in Jerusalem at the time it occurred. Why is there no report from the opposing Jews proving that it didn't happen? My guess is that they had no proof that could refute the evidence presented by the Christian believers."

"So, in your mind history does not disprove anything about the life, times, and teachings of Jesus," my son chimes in.

"That is true."

"Talk to me about another branch of science."

"Let's talk about physics. The work of Albert Einstein, the recent work of Stephen Wolfram, and the scientists working with DNA do not disprove the teachings in the Bible. I believe they all shed light on how God built this wonderful universe, but none of their theories really conflict with the Bible. Their work is wonderful and very helpful to improve our physical existence. I am, like most people, very grateful for their efforts.

"So ..." I continued, "let's talk about archaeology. Archaeology has been a great friend of Christianity for many years. The findings of ancient copies of the Bible in the caves of Qumran in Israel, in 1947, supported and reinforced completely the accuracy of the Bible. The discovery of the correct location of Mt. Sinai in Saudi Arabia removes one of the debatable issues in archaeology in favor of Christianity. I'm eager for archaeologists to continue their work and discoveries. They continue to provide new and confirm old evidence supporting the accuracy of the Bible.

"Fourth Consideration: *Jesus' followers, during His time on earth, did not live perfect Jesus-like lives.* This is an encouragement to me. Jesus continued to love His disciples despite their failings. Love and forgiveness are unique dimensions of the Christian faith and says a great deal about the God we serve.

"Fifth Consideration: *Christians of today do not live*

perfect Jesus-like lives after they become Christians.
However, many people use this as an excuse for dismissing
or even trying to get to know about Christianity. They watch
each week as professional athletes make mistakes in their
areas of expertise. They read about movie stars making
mistakes in their careers and personal lives. They quickly
forgive these athletes and celebrities for their humanness,
but they wait for an opportunity to pounce on a Christian
who errs. People who are adherents to any other religion are
not subjected to the same criticism and hostility. It is a
double standard. The double standard exists because people
who are against Christianity are rejecting God and working
hard to justify their rejection, but they still feel guilty. I have
much hope they will accept the truth.

"Sixth Consideration: *Christianity is the most, if not the
only, maligned and mocked religion in the general media.*
Isn't it interesting to you that of all the political and religious leaders in all of history, only one name gets used as a
swear word on television, on radio, and in the movies? How
quickly would you or I be stopped and soundly chastised by
almost anyone and everyone if we used any other religious
leader's name, such as Muhammad, Gandhi, or Buddha, as a
swear word. Even the vulgar radio and TV talk show hosts
are not brave enough to do that. They know that some of the
followers of these other leaders might cause them serious
physical harm.

"Followers of Jesus Christ have learned to cringe and
whisper a prayer of 'God forgive them' under their breath.
Why do these vulgar radio and TV talk show people use His
name as a swear word? Out of their ignorance, this has now
become habit. Is Jesus persecuted today? I am certain He is
and this gross misuse of His name is a blaring example. The
fact that He is singled out adds further credence that He is
the One True God."

"Why don't Christians get more active in trying to stop

the misuse of Jesus' name?"

"I think the reason is twofold. Christians don't believe their objections would convince anyone to quit. And—it's just easier to forgive and pray these people will eventually accept the truth. When they do, they'll feel as bad as everyone else who has done it before, during, or after they accept the Truth of Jesus."

"Dad, you don't sound as though you are angry about these things although it seems you could be. Why aren't you angry?"

"I'm not angry because anger would be a waste of effort. Also, I believe it is helpful for me to think of all people as being on a path to knowing the Truth about the One True God. My job is to help them along the path. Some appear to be going in the opposite direction. Some appear to be going to the right or to the left. My responsibility is to seek the things that I might do to get them going forward in the right direction. I don't think being angry with them helps in any way. I want to do what I can to get them to begin exploring the evidence and let the words of God, along with many prayers, lead them to the Truth. I know that formula works. It worked for me."

Hope and Expectations

My son nods, and I move on to the next topic.

"I can't avoid thinking about how something impacts me if I believe it or try to incorporate it into my life. For example, if I eat and exercise properly, I will be doing something good for my physical body. If I help others, I am more likely to receive help. If I pay attention to others while driving on the road and follow the rules, I'm less likely to have a serious accident."

"I know those are true statements, but how do they fit in with this discussion about God and how people perceive Him?"

"If I accept the notion that evolution explains the origin of man, what good does that do me? I see myself as a temporal, physical event that will die, decompose, and become dust again. That does not motivate or encourage me in any way. It steals the meaning from life."

"Yes, but non-believing people can still live good lives and be good to others."

"Yes they can, but what is their primary motivation and what are their private thoughts? In tough situations, they must feel pretty lonely. Even in the best of times, they are likely to feel a great deal of futility. And I find it impossible to believe that they wouldn't sense reasonable doubt in regard to their conviction that there is no life after death— no hope or expectation beyond themselves. That seems like an empty existence to me. I don't wish that on anyone. So if people really do believe that way, why would they want others to think like they do? They offer their potential fellow believers nothing. Well, they offer them a moment of thinking they are an intellectual superior, even though it is false. They are simply being rebellious and obstinate. They have no facts to support their position. They do an elaborate dance around an abundance of facts and evidence."

"It does sound a bit empty."

"If I offer someone a belief in a beautiful set of rules to live by with the low expectation that I can avoid, after death, being recycled into a worse life circumstance, what value is that to them? If it's all people know, they will do it because they know nothing else. But I *do* know the truth, and I can compare the truth with their alternative. I am obligated to do all I can to encourage them to let me share the truth, so they can share and live in the hope that I have."

"Why do you feel obligated to share your belief in Jesus with others?"

I lean toward my son and speak with passion and gentleness. "At first I felt obligated because the Bible says that it's every Christian's duty—we call it the Great Commission. But, now that I understand it better, I see what Jesus and the Holy Spirit do for me each day. How can I help but want that for others. I want it especially for my family and friends, but I also want it for people I meet and people I hope to meet."

"You sound serious about sharing your faith. You make it seem urgent."

"If I try to get others to accept a personal relationship with a living God who loves them and who will become part of their lives, then I offer something of value that is of immediate help. And look what else they would receive—the assurance of a spectacular eternal life that promises that when their physical body turns to dust, their spiritual body will soar in the heavens. That is a hope worth sharing with everyone I meet. It's a hope and a dependable promise that demands to be shared!"

The Decision is Made

Almost without taking a breath, I continue. "I'm always concerned when I hear people say, 'I'll make a decision about God and the issues of the universe at another time.' Maybe they're waiting to get more or different information or are expecting an event to occur that will bring instant clarity to their confusion."

"Why do you think they are confused?"

"I believe people who are waiting to make a decision or commitment are unsettled. They don't know what to do, so they postpone their decision. That's a sign of confusion to me."

"No, no, I meant what are they confused about?"

"Oh, sorry, I guess I was eager to make that point. I have more to say on that, but I'll get back to it after I've answered your question. God and the universe are very complex issues. Most people don't try to understand or resolve them. Instead, they take the path of least resistance."

"So, if it's confusing because of its actual complexity, how do people make decisions?"

"Almost all decisions are made with incomplete or 'not enough' information. That doesn't mean the complete information isn't available—it's just not available to that person about that issue at that time. When this occurs, people scout and flirt around with ideas and people until they find a place that is comfortable for them. The comfort or 'fit' is usually first defined in their social context and then the person adjusts or 'rewords' their values and principles to assure and accommodate the needed social 'fit'. People get into gangs, churches, and intellectual circles using the same process."

"You sound a bit negative and cynical."

"I'm not negative. It seems that is the way it happens. People don't usually emphasize their beliefs no matter what may come. They emphasize their wanting to belong and this is where the problem arises."

"What problem?"

"Oh, yes, I have jumped back to the problem of postponing a decision. Postponing a decision about accepting Jesus as God and Savior does not place one in a neutral place where there is 'no harm, no foul'. Choosing 'not to accept' Jesus and being committed to Him is a decision to join the other team. There is no neutral place. Too many people are delaying with the expectation that they will be able to make a choice at the right time or in the last moment of time.

"Some of them believe their 'neutral' place will be good enough. They are using the excuse of needing more information, but I believe they are avoiding the decision to avoid social discomfort. All the information anyone needs is available, clearly and bluntly. There are no efforts to conceal or make the truths of the Bible complicated or mysterious. Bibles are available everywhere. They are accurately translated and written in modern language. The message and meaning is consistent with the message and meaning at the time it was written.

"People may ask, 'yes, but what about the other religions and their books?'. If a person asks and then makes no attempt to read, study, and explore, that person will remain confused. 'I was confused', is not an acceptable excuse. This only serves to keep a person in a state of indecision, and the absence of a decision is a decision to reject God."

"People don't mean to reject God."

"I agree. But the reality is that we live in a world in which God allows us to have free will and choice. If we don't use that right of choice to choose Him, the end result will not be good."

"What do you believe is the 'bad end result' for those who don't choose Jesus?"

"I need to say again that I accept the Bible as the accurate words of God and, in it, He has given us all the information we need to make good choices. In the Bible, Jesus teaches that those who do not accept Him will be cast into a lake of fire. In the teaching it is clear that the lake of fire was not used as a metaphor; it is a literal lake of fire."

"So, you are certain people who die without accepting Jesus go to an eternal existence in a lake of fire?"

"Yes, I am," I answer slowly and sadly.

"How can a loving and merciful God send people to that kind of outrageous torture?"

"I don't know. I don't understand it, and I can't explain it—neither can I explain it away. That's what He said. If I accept the other teachings, I also have to accept this one. The Bible is not a menu; we can't pick the parts that suit us. It is a very concise book—a summary—and yet it contains all we need to know."

"How does that make you feel about what God is really like? He says and does all these good and kind things and then throws in this literal burning hell?"

"I can't possibly understand the mind of God. I believe it is counter-productive to add further speculation and doubt about the issue of a literal hell. The decision is to choose Him or not choose Him. I choose Him because of the evidence and promises He has provided, not because of the fear of an outrageous penalty. Other people may choose to ignore the evidence. Some seem to want to reason all this away, because they entertain a conflicting set of ideas. Many are completely repulsed by the idea of hell and use that to reject God—as if that would somehow change His mind."

"You sound a little like you don't think it's your problem, and you don't need to address it."

"Please forgive me for giving you that impression. It is my problem, and I am addressing it."

"How are you addressing it?"

"I'm praying for specific people everyday that they will be open to the words and promises of God through Jesus. Two scenes come to my mind. One is that of a wick in a candle. I can't imagine what it would feel like to be a wick, but that is an image I have of a person in hell. I have never met or heard about a person I would want to suffer that torment.

"The second image is the closing scene in the movie *Schindler's List*. In that scene there are more than a thousand people that Schindler has just saved from being killed in a vicious manner by the Nazis. As they hand Schindler a small gold ring as a 'thank you' and 'reminder', all he can think about is he could have saved one more if he had had that gold ring sooner. I pray all Christians have the heart of Schindler, which is also the heart of Jesus. I seek each day to help one more person choose Jesus. Given what I am certain about, it would be terrible of me not to help every day. I'm motivated partly because I don't want a single person to be a wick for eternity and partly because I know their lives will be better while they're alive on earth."

I pause and look at my son.

"Dad, I don't know what to say."

"Then consider this. No one gets off this planet alive. After we die, we're either going to heaven or hell. Let's get everyone to choose Jesus and go to heaven."

There is silence as we both feel the heaviness of this part of the conversation.

Then my son breaks the silence. "Dad, you say that with sincerity and conviction, but it sounds almost too simple."

"Why is it too simple?"

"It sounds almost silly to say 'let's get everyone to choose Jesus and go to Heaven.'"

"I think the reason it sounds silly is that it addresses such a simple foundational need and truth that you feel we should say more to make it sound more intelligent. I submit to you that our present culture is so focused on sounding intelligent that clear, simple and truthful is out of style. Our colleges and universities stress a need for complexity and that complexity is a 'friend' of knowledge. Complexity is not a 'friend' of wisdom. Wisdom can always be expressed in a simple way. The wisdom we're talking about here is, 'let's get people to choose Jesus and go to heaven.' Let's get them to focus long enough to discover and grasp the truths of the Bible. With these truths, they will not be confused by the false alternatives that keep causing them to put off choosing Jesus. It is that simple."

"Do you really think it is that simple?"

"I do."

The Close

❧

"Dad, I have one last question. 'How do you respond to the intellectual types who disagree with what you're teaching'?"

"My first thought is to silently pray for love and wisdom to guide my responses. I stay focused on the abundance of clear and simple evidence available to support the truths of Christianity. I refuse to participate in speculation about distracting issues, which I find is the major tactic of most skeptics. And I don't expect each discussion or disagreement to end in agreement. I'm always just pleased to have an opportunity to share the evidence."

"I wish I had taken notes today," my son says. "It has been great. I really feel I heard your heart and mind. I know you've studied a lot over many years, and I admire that. That alone makes it easier for me to have this conversation. You've put a lot of effort into knowing what and why you believe certain things. Too many people seem to just parrot back what they've been told. You inspire me, Pop."

We both laugh. I know when I hear 'Pop' that all is good between us.

"I've made some notes, and I have a few others at

home," I answer. "Tell you what—I'm going to write it all down for you as well as I can. We could have talked about many more things, and I could have shared much more evidence of the existence of God, but time doesn't allow it today. I'll give you a list of books from which you can get more details. Today we have only scratched the surface. After I finish writing this for you, will you look through it and give me your thoughts?"

"Sure. I'd be glad to do that."

"It'll take me a month or so, but I'll get it done. I want to write it down so those I know and love will make wise decisions using readily available evidence. I don't want them distracted in their understanding or decision making by speculative questioning about 'unknowable' and 'unanswerable' things."

Never has a lunch seemed so wonderful. The Last Supper of Jesus with His disciples now means a whole lot more to me than it ever has. It is a lunch we will always remember.

Resources

Many other books, articles, and websites could have been included in this list. It was my intention to provide an adequate, rather than an intimidating or overwhelming set of resources for the reader, as he or she sets out to become well informed about God and the life of faith.

Books

The Holy Bible

In Search of the Mountain of God: The Discovery of the Real Mt. Sinai by Robert Cornuke and David Halbrook. Nashville: Broadman & Holman Publishers, 2000.

Josephus a Unique Witness by David Bentley-Taylor. Geanies House, Fearn, Ross-shire, IV20 1TW, Great Britain: Christian Focus Publications, 1999.

Surprised by the Power of the Holy Spirit by Jack Deere. Grand Rapids: Zondervan Publishing House, 1993.

The Discovery of Genesis by C.H. Kang, and Ethel R Nelson. St. Louis: Concordia Publishing House, 1979.

The New Evidence That Demands a Verdict by Josh D. McDowell. Nashville: Thomas Nelson Publishers, 1999.

Handbook of Today's Religions by Josh D. McDowell and Don Stewart. Nashville: Thomas Nelson Publishers, 1983.

The Darwin Legend by James Moore. Grand Rapids: Baker Books, 1994.

The Case for a Creator by Lee Strobel. Grand Rapids: Zondervan, 2004.

The Case for Christ by Lee Strobel. Grand Rapids: Zondervan Publishing House, 1998.

A New Kind of Science by Stephen Wolfram. Champaign: Wolfram Media, Inc., 2002.

Jesus Among Other Gods by Ravi Zacharias. Nashville: W Publishing Group, a Division of Thomas Nelson, Inc., 2000.

Websites
www.barna.org The Barna Research Group
www.baseinstitute.org Bible Archaeology Search and Exploration Institute
www.icr.org Institute for Creation Research
www.josh.org Josh McDowell Ministry
www.rzim.org Ravi Zacharias International Ministries

Seminar
www.dwainecanovaministries.com
Dwaine Canova Ministries provides a one-day seminar covering this topic in more detail. The purpose of the seminar is to help believers understand the material in more depth, strengthen their faith, and prepare them to present a logical explanation of what they believe in a loving, courteous, and respectful manner.

Printed in the United States
22531LVS00001B/79-225